Early Baptists

John Smyth, Thomas Helwys and the Quest for Religious Liberty

By

Stephen Greasley

British Library Cataloguing in Publication Data.
A catalogue record for this book is available
from the British Library.

ISBN 978 086071 632 7

Commissioned Publication of

23 Park Road, Ilkeston, Derbys DE7 5DA
Tel: 0115 932 0643 www.moorleys.co.uk

TRIBUTE

This book is dedicated to Dr Barrie (Barrington) White, tutor in Church History 1963 – 1972 and Principal of Regents Park College, Oxford 1972 – 1989.

Barrie White made major contributions to the study of Baptist history, perhaps most significantly his study of the English Separatist Tradition which is a starting point for most students and scholars of early English Separatism.

Generations of students at Regents Park College were taught by this thoroughgoing English gentleman. My fondest memories of Dr White are his quaint enquiry as to the welfare of "your lady"; his mildest of rebukes that my start of term examination "bore all the hallmarks of a honeymoon vacation"; his pride and fascination with the portrait, and life, of William Kiffin; leading worship in College Chapel with his Geneva gown; and his charming grace at the beginning of all College meals: "for the gifts of your grace and the fellowship of this College, we praise your name O God."

For all that Barrie White has given to the Baptist denomination; for his humour, charm, example, and scholarship, we praise your name O God.

Derby
July 2009

i

Dr Barrington White

ACKNOWLEDGEMENTS

January 2009 marked the 21st Anniversary of my ordination to the Baptist ministry. Consequently this allowed me the privilege of taking a third period of sabbatical leave. I am grateful to Pear Tree Road Baptist Church, Derby for allowing me nine weeks free of Sunday responsibilities during which time I was able to carry out much of the research into this book. I am also grateful to the Ministry Department of the Baptist Union of Great Britain for a bursary grant towards the cost of travel and book purchases, while a generous grant from the Whitley Lectureship Committee has made the publication of this volume possible.

The research involved in this study was only possible because of the access to some world class library facilities. I would, therefore, like to place on record my indebtedness to Emma Walsh and Sheila Wood at Regents Park College's Angus Library. Their kind assistance has been very much appreciated. I am also deeply indebted to Jennie Lynch at the Parliamentary Archives for retrieving the early Baptist document 'A Most Humble Supplication'; to Geoffrey Thorndike Martin and Jane Gregory of Christ's College, Cambridge for kindly making available material on John Smyth; to the staff at the University of Nottingham's Manuscripts and Special Collections department for access to the Archdeaconry presentment bills; and last but by no means least to Liz Tisdall, Archivist at Carey Baptist College, Auckland, New Zealand, who managed to unearth the article by J.T.Crozier on Joan Helwys. I was impressed.

Indeed it is probably worth pointing out at this stage what a tremendous improvement to historical research has come about through the World Wide Web. The ease with which people can be contacted, answers gleaned, information exchanged, has made research so much easier. The facility to track down and obtain long out of print books through Amazon and Alibris, (or local book stores like Scarthins of Cromford) not to mention the amount of online publications and historical information available at the click of a button is truly amazing. I refer in the book at several points to ways of accessing rare sixteenth and seventeenth century literature all of which has been made possible through the world of the internet and Google.

Back on planet earth, useful information has been made available through good local studies sections of libraries, the Worksop Library being especially good in this regard. The Bassetlaw Museum at Amcott House, Retford, has some good material on the Pilgrim Fathers, as does Gainsborough Old Hall which is always worth a visit, being so intimately connected with the Smyth Helwys Separatists. Visitors to the East Midlands may well enjoy the 'Mayflower Trail' which takes in many of the sites associated with the early Separatists. All Saints Church, Babworth is well worth a visit in that connection, although I was struck by the irony that the Church is at the forefront of the movement to safeguard the Book of Common Prayer which was the one thing Richard Clyfton and the Babworth Separatists wanted to be free of!!

Tried and trusted colleagues Douglas Wooldridge and Derek Meller have proved more than helpful in giving me access to material from the East Midlands Archives and their own private collections. New colleagues have also proved a real boon this year, chief among these being Sue Allan, whose studies on Gainsborough Old Hall, the Hickman family, and the early Separatists proved most helpful; and Dr Jeremy Bangs who kindly shared with me some of the fruit of his own extensive research into the Pilgrim Fathers. Dr James Coggins and Dr Ian Randall, who have trodden this path themselves, made some valuable suggestions; while Professor John Briggs has pointed me in the right direction from time to time. Dr Peter Shepherd has also read the proofs of this book with great thoroughness and for this I am especially grateful.

It would be churlish of me if I did not express thanks to my wife, Sharon, and daughter, Rachael who have humoured me in my fascination with the characters and themes of this book. My son, David, as ever has proved a reassuring presence when it came to some of the more technical aspects of producing the book, while Moorleys of Ilkeston are to be commended for their sterling work in getting the text fit for publication, and their brilliant cover design.

For all these people, and a host of others who have contributed in various ways, I am truly grateful.

Stephen Greasley

CONTENTS

INTRODUCTION

In 1609 John Smyth formed the first English Baptist Church (albeit in Amsterdam!) In 1612 Thomas Helwys formed the first Baptist Church on English soil. It was at Spitalfields, just outside the city boundary of London. We are now some 400 years on from these events. Smyth and Helwys were pioneers. English Baptist History finds a beginning with them. Yet, today their names are hardly known at all, even within Baptist congregations.

This book makes no great claim to originality. There will be little here that hasn't been in the public domain for a very long time. But what it does try to do is to make available material that in many instances was produced nearly a hundred years ago and which is no longer accessible except to the research student and the visitor to great libraries. It also tries to bring some clarity to issues that are muddled, speculative and contradictory in those earlier studies. And the book will also attempt to draw together material from very different areas of study. Smyth and Helwys, for example, were part of the early Separatists from Nottinghamshire and Lincolnshire, some of whom were to become the Pilgrim Fathers who settled in America. They feature, therefore, (although not as much as they should do) in the various studies about the Pilgrim Fathers that are still being produced. But Smyth and Helwys also appear in the histories of the seventeenth century English refugee communities in Holland as well as the general histories of English Baptists. Much of this study is an attempt to cull material from each of these areas and to provide a more comprehensive and focused assessment of these two men.

So often Smyth and Helwys have appeared as minor characters in someone else's History. They have featured as incidental figures. This in part reflects the fact that they represent a minority voice in the Separatist movement, the part that pushed further the logic of withdrawing from a corrupt Church and saw a need to start everything afresh – including baptism. Out of embarrassment for this extreme fringe, writers have often tried to airbrush Smyth and Helwys out of the script, and to pretend either that they were not there or that they did not matter.[1]

This book, on the other hand, tries to put Smyth and Helwys centre stage; to rehabilitate them. Thomas Helwys was to obtain a degree of fame for some things he wrote about freedom of conscience and freedom of religion in his last work, 'The Mystery of Iniquity'. A modern generation has latched onto ideas featured in that work because they resonate with meaning in our own society where, in a very different context, issues of religious freedom and freedom for minorities are again becoming important. But arguably for both Smyth and Helwys the battle that mattered to them most by the time of their deaths was the battle with Calvinism and, for Smyth in particular, the crucial role free will should play in the development of a meaningful and liberating theology.

Thomas Helwys parted company with John Smyth in 1610. They disagreed on aspects of doctrine and Church practice that made it impossible for them to collaborate any further. Helwys went so far as to excommunicate his former Pastor. In truth, however, they were much closer together than Helwys was willing to acknowledge. On the fundamentals of their faith, and their passionate belief that men and women are not morally and spiritually impotent, Smyth and Helwys were in agreement. For that reason alone their names should be twinned together.

The spiritual journey both men travelled was so rapid that few were able to keep pace with them. They changed their views with alacrity, so much so that they were frequently accused of muddled and inconsistent thought. Smyth was the theologian; Helwys the country squire. The latter certainly looked to the former for a theological lead. But when it came to the crunch, Helwys was able to hold his ground, and was able to articulate his own theological positions and move beyond his teacher and mentor.

Ironically, just as their minority status among Separatists and Congregationalists assured they were ignored by generations of those who studied this formative period, equally their minority status among

English and American Baptists, shaped more by Calvinism than Smyth and Helwys' gentler Arminianism, destined them to a place in the religious wilderness.

John Smyth and Thomas Helwys are never likely to become household names after this length of time. But a better understanding of who they were and what they believed might well contribute to an increase in theological literacy in the twenty first century Church, and hopefully make a fragmented and incoherent story that much clearer.

At times, when I have tried to explain to people what this project has been about, I have felt a little uneasy. Describing religious battles that happened 400 years ago not only brings a cloud of mist over people's faces but it makes me sound like some religious dinosaur. In our current ecumenical climate do we really need to drag up the tarnished record of our predecessors? The world has moved on; the Church has moved on; we all face much different challenges than those of Smyth and Helwys. So why take us back there?

The simple and honest answer might be that I enjoy history and I enjoy this piece of history. But more profoundly I do believe that the answers to so many of the Church's present problems, for example relevance, mission, and pluralism, ultimately have solutions which are theological. And surprisingly I think that as we try to delve deeper into our understanding of God and the nature of mission in the twenty first century we will find ourselves once again returning to the fundamental questions that divided our forefathers and foremothers.

There are those who immerse themselves in the history of the past because they find the past more congenial than the present. It is a form of escapism. But for others, in order to be able to deal with the modern world and its challenges for the Church, we have to comprehend where we have come from. Raking over old battles isn't, I trust, a return to the ecclesiastical cold war, but is a way of helping us move forward into a new future which will, in my opinion, be one of unprecedented ecumenical consolidation. But we will only be able to embrace that new ecumenical future if we are fully aware of the journey that has already been travelled.

Footnote

1. One of the most prominent Pilgrim Fathers, William Bradford, in his 'Of Plymouth Plantation' (p.9) makes only a passing and dismissive mention to John Smyth. Acknowledging Smyth to be a "man of able gifts and a good preacher" he says that Smyth and his followers "falling into some errors in the Low Countries, there (for the most part) buried themselves and their names."More recently, the Concise Dictionary of National Biography (OUP 1992) said of Smyth that his religious views and tracts were "incoherent and distracted." That is hardly fair and hardly objective.

CHAPTER 1

ANABAPTISM AND THE EUROPEAN BACKGROUND

On 21st January 1525 George Blaurock, a former Roman Catholic priest, was baptised by Conrad Grebel in the home of Felix Mantz in Zurich. The movement that became known as Anabaptism was born. Anabaptism simply means 'baptised again.' For decades it was employed as a term of abuse. Only later was it adopted as a badge of honour.

The events of that January evening were the culmination of a fairly lengthy process of thought and debate. Ulrich Zwingli, the Swiss Protestant Reformer, had encouraged groups of young men to meet together to reflect on the scriptures and to determine the policy and direction of the Protestant Reformation in Switzerland. Zwingli himself had pioneered a novel, memorialist view of the sacraments which encouraged some of his students to go further in their assessment. In the weeks prior to the evening of 21st January Zwingli and Bullinger had been engaged in debates with some students who questioned the slow pace of reformation in the city, and who, in particular, doubted the validity of infant baptism. Having opened this Pandora's box, and being fearful of the consequences such a position might have with the city authorities, Zwingli attempted to put the lid back on. He banned future discussion of the matter, and the authorities banned all such meetings. But it was too late.

A Church of (re)baptised believers was convened at Zollikon, five miles from Zurich, consisting of 35 converts. The civil authorities in St. Gall adopted a tolerant approach to the new teaching, and in April Conrad Grebel was able to preach for two weeks before baptising large numbers of people in the river on Palm Sunday 1525. At the same time William Reublin, one of the emissaries of the new Swiss Anabaptists, visited Waldshut just outside Switzerland, where there was already great interest in the new thinking. Even before January 21st Balthasar Hubmaier had been writing against the practice of baptising children and urging instead that a simple act of blessing should be performed.

Reublin shared with the crowds in Waldshut the momentous events in Zurich and Zollikon with the result that on Easter Sunday 1525 Hubmaier and sixty others accepted re-baptism at Reublin's hands. In the days that followed Hubmaier went on to re-baptise 300 people using a milk bucket with water from a fountain in the town square.

The following year Hubmaier arrived in Augsburg where he found a group of people around John Denck who were already predisposed to Anabaptist practice. In May 1526 Hubmaier baptised Denck and a number of others. Before the month was out Denck had baptised John (Hans) Hut who in the coming months took the new message by word and in writing to Austria.

The spread of Anabaptism was, however, anything but smooth. Its advocates advanced at great personal risk in the face of implacable opposition from Catholic and Protestant alike. The first Baptist martyr was Hippolytus Eberli[1] who was burned at the stake in the Catholic Swiss Canton of Schwyz on 29th May 1525. Conrad Grebel, one of the original triumvirate, died of the plague in August 1526. His father, however, Jacob Grebel, who had adopted his son's views, was beheaded at the Zurich fish market on 13th October 1526. A month later the Zurich council passed a law attaching the death penalty to acts of re-baptism and attendance at Baptist preaching. Mantz and Blaurock were arrested and imprisoned. Mantz was judicially drowned on 5th January 1527, the first martyr at Protestant hands. Blaurock, who was not a native of Zurich, was merely beaten with rods through the town and banished for life. Blaurock subsequently moved to Austria taking charge of an Anabaptist fellowship in the Tyrol. He was burned at the stake on September 6th 1529 near Klausen. John Hut was seized in September 1527. He was tortured, racked and then returned to his prison cell whereupon a candle left by his guard tipped over and he burned to death. The South German authorities, not to be denied their pound of flesh, ordered that his dead body should still be brought back into court. It was tied to the chair in court, and formally condemned to be burned at the stake the next day. Balthasar Hubmaier was arrested in Austria. On 3rd March 1528 he was racked and tortured but refused to recant his views. On the 10th March he was burned alive in Vienna.

Three days later his wife was executed by drowning in the river Danube.

The cause and reputation of Anabaptism suffered irreparable damage through the debacle of Munster. This north German city became a haven and a magnet for Anabaptists throughout northern Europe in the early 1530s. Under the charismatic leadership first of John Mathijs and then John Beukels (of Leiden), the commune adopted draconian measures to enforce its ethical-religious policies. Blasphemy, seditious language, backbiting and even complaining were punishable by death. All property was held in common; marriage was made compulsory, and polygamy was encouraged. After months of siege and famine, the city was taken in June 1535 by Imperial troops. Fearful reprisals were exacted on the survivors, but it was the damage to the image of Anabaptism that was the most devastating. For city elders and princes alike the cause of Anabaptism was inextricably linked to the excesses of Munster. Little sympathy was to be found for those sincere believers who simply wished to follow the dictates of conscience. Anabaptism was seen as a major threat to civil order, and it was severely crushed wherever it was found.

It was to take more than a generation before the shadow of Munster began to retreat from the public mind, and it was to take some careful and measured thinking from Anabaptists for the damage to be undone. One of the main contributors to this theological renaissance of Anabaptism was Menno Simons.

Born in 1496 in West Frisia, Menno Simons was ordained a Roman Catholic priest in 1524. He had suffered doubts over crucial aspects of that Church's teaching, including transubstantiation and infant baptism, well before he left the parish priesthood in January 1536. The following year he was (re)baptised and took pastoral charge of a beleaguered group of Anabaptists. Constantly dogged by the authorities Menno Simons led a wanderer's existence, visiting the scattered groups of Anabaptists, catechising, baptising and building up the churches wherever he went. He married in 1536 or 1537 but for many years had no fixed abode.

For two years Simons ministered in Amsterdam where, in spite of the constant threat of arrest, he managed to write books and tracts which were to be of major importance. 'The Spiritual Resurrection' (1536) and 'The New Birth' (1537) explore his most passionate concern for human and spiritual regeneration, with the consequent ethical outworking of this in holiness. "All those who are born and regenerated from above out of God, through the living Word, are also of the mind and disposition and have the same aptitude for good that He has of whom they were born and begotten."[2] "In your life you must be so converted and changed that you become new men in Christ, so that Christ is in you, and you are in Christ."[3] Menno disagreed fundamentally with Martin Luther that man is justified by faith alone. The Anabaptist leader was insistent that faith and fruits are inseparable.[4]There could be no saving faith that was not demonstrated by holiness of life. The Christian must truly be 'conformed unto Christ.'[5]One of Menno's other major contributions to Anabaptist thinking was his insistence upon the implementation of Church discipline on erring brethren. 'A kind admonition on Church discipline' (1541) adopts a compassionate and pastorally sensitive tone to this vexed question. To preserve the holiness of the Church there has to be gentle admonition and brotherly instruction to those who are going astray in order to guide them back into the right ways. In extreme cases excommunication ('The Ban') may need to be imposed with heavy hearts, and such a person may need to be shunned where stubborn refusal to accept the discipline of the Church is encountered. But, said Menno, "we do not want to expel any, but rather to receive; not to amputate, but rather to heal; not to discard, but rather to win back; not to grieve, but rather to comfort; not to condemn, but rather to save. For this is the true nature of a Christian brother."[6]

In 1543 he left Holland and spent the remaining eighteen years of his life ministering in northern Germany and the Baltic seacoast region. Such was his standing and influence that he gave his name to that strand of biblical Anabaptist teaching known as the Mennonites. Simons died in January 1561. The last years of his life were dogged by controversy between the Anabaptist fellowships in Holland and north Germany regarding the imposition of excommunication. There were serious disagreements as to how strictly the Ban should be enforced.

If Menno Simons was the leading figure amongst the north German Anabaptists then Pilgram Marpeck was his equivalent in south Germany. Trained as a mining engineer, Marpeck espoused his Anabaptist views in Strasburg. Following a series of debates with Martin Bucer he was eventually driven out of the city. From 1545 until his death in December 1556 he lived in Augsburg where his Anabaptist views were mildly tolerated by the city authorities. His valuable service as city engineer saved him from the harassment many of his contemporaries suffered, and it was from this position of relative tranquillity that Marpeck was able to produce some of his important literary works.

His 'Confession of Faith'[7] was presented to the City Council of Strasburg in January 1532. One of its main ideas was that the state should have no role in the religious settlement of the land. While the state had a legitimate sphere of influence, it had no right to encroach on the Kingdom of Christ. The Church should be free of political interference to determine its policy and direction. Marpeck's 'Admonition' of 1542 provides his most eloquent defence of believers' baptism. He considered infant baptism as preliminary to the destruction of all notions of a holy Church. But believers' baptism itself was no panacea of the Church's ills. "It is a comparatively simple thing to thrust someone into water or to pour water over him; indeed it does the soul no good nor is pollution of the flesh removed."[8] Baptism saves us, said Marpeck, only when it is combined with a sincere conscience. "Otherwise baptism is of no use and is only a mockery in the presence of God."[9]

Most interesting and illuminating are Marpeck's letters in which much of his theologising was worked out. Writing, for example, to the Swiss Brethren in 1531, Marpeck felt the need to tackle the perennial and thorny issue of the implementation of Church discipline and the Ban. Believing that some of his Swiss colleagues were a little too quick to judgment, Marpeck reminded them that Jesus said "By their fruits you shall know them" and not by their leaves and blossom!![10] Give people time to mature and to grow, he maintained. Don't expect perfection too early.

There were inevitably disagreements between the different Anabaptists. Some, like Hut, were driven by an apocalyptic mindset which anticipated the imminent return of Christ. Hut proved to be quite a divisive figure amongst the German Anabaptists. Michael Servetus developed views on the Trinity which did not coincide with the majority of his colleagues, while Melchior Hofmann developed Christological views (the celestial flesh of Christ) which did attract growing interest amongst Anabaptists for generations to come.

Jacob Widemann and Jacob Hutter insisted that communion of property was a natural outworking of both the Gospel and the fellowship of the Christian Church. Dozens of Anabaptist communes or households were established in Moravia throughout the 1530s until Hutter was martyred at Innsbruck on February 24th 1536. This practice of common ownership of property was fiercely denounced by other Anabaptists, the most vocal being Balthasar Hubmaier.

Hubmaier himself made a passionate defence of the right of Christians to bear arms and the need for Christian magistrates ('On the Sword' 1527).[11] In this belief, however, he was decidedly in the minority. Both Marpeck and Menno Simons came down strongly against Christians participating in judicial and military administration. Christians, said Menno, "are the children of peace who have beaten their swords into ploughshares and their spears into pruning hooks, and know war no more. They give to Caesar the things that are Caesar's and to God the things that are God's."[12] Jesus' Kingdom was not of this world. We must love our enemies. How can we do that if we are charged with the implementation of the law, and the punishment of wrong-doers?

The Anabaptists parted company with the Protestant Reformers Luther, Zwingli and Calvin over several issues. Salvation could not simply be by faith alone, insisted the Anabaptists, it had to be demonstrated by palpable life-change. While all the Anabaptists were committed to the Bible, several leading Anabaptists wished to distance themselves from the Bibliolatry that was perceived to be taking place within Lutheranism. John (Hans) Denck, for example, refused to refer to the Bible as The Word of God, a title he felt was only appropriate for Jesus himself. The Scriptures, Denck maintained, were only a material witness to Christ.[13]The human Jesus played a key role in the theology of the early Anabaptists who considered the aim of the Christian life to be conformity to His image. The Anabaptists also reacted to the "paralysing Augustinianism of Luther."[14] They developed a very different anthropology to Luther, objecting to the pessimism of his teaching and his wholly negative view of human potentiality. Hubmaier, for example, accepted that the human body and soul were dead through sin, but insisted that the spirit within each person was capable of responding to the invitation of the Gospel. "For what purpose are all the invitations of the Gospel if man cannot possibly heed them?"[15] Instead of the determinism of Protestant thinking Hubmaier steadfastly maintained the inviolability of human freedom. "Whoever denies the freedom of the human will denies and rejects more than half of the Holy Scriptures."[16] "He who denies the free will of man and calls it an empty claim, is nothing in himself, nicknames God a tyrant, charges Him with injustice, and gives the wicked excuse to remain in their sins."[17]

The other major theological difference between the Protestant Reformers and the Anabaptists was over the concept of the Church, and alongside that the relationship of the state to the Church. The Protestant Reformers were keen to employ the services of the state in imposing a religious settlement. Unity and uniformity were central to their notion of a Christian society. By contrast the Anabaptists found the concept of a Christian society quite alien. They worked with a very different model of Church (a voluntary gathering of believers) and believed that it necessitated being free from all political interference or coercion. The Schleitheim Confession[18] of 1527 made it plain not only that separation from the world was a foundation of the true Christian community, but also that pastors of churches should be supported simply by the gifts of the congregation. They should in no way be paid by the state or regarded as servants of the state.

There was a natural corollary to this concept of human freedom, and of freedom from the state. This was the exercise of religious freedom. The Anabaptists' commitment to religious freedom came not from expediency or self interest, but rather out of theological and philosophical conviction. Since the only religion that was of any value was that which was freely chosen, it followed that any form of religious coercion was, by definition, self defeating. Only by persuasion could a person be led to the truth. The exercise of religious liberty was fundamental to the practice of true religion. Denck put this well in his commentary on the Prophet Micah: "I stand fast on what the prophet says here. Everyone among all peoples, may move around in the name of his God. That is to say, no-one shall deprive another – whether Heathen or Jew or Christian, but rather allow everyone to move in all territories in the name of his God. So may we benefit in the peace which God gives."[19]

It was Balthasar Hubmaier, however, who was to provide the finest defence of religious liberty. Writing before his (re)baptism, Hubmaier was appalled at the level of violence meted out against Christians in the name of God. "Concerning heretics and those who burn them"(1524)[20] was a masterpiece of religious writing. He begins by insisting that the real heretics are those who refuse to heed the Holy Scriptures. One of those Scriptures he has in mind is the Parable of the Wheat and the Tares. In this Parable Jesus insists that the wheat and tares should be allowed to grow together. They will eventually be gathered on the Day of Judgement at which point due punishment will be made. But no such judgement and punishment should be made before that, and certainly not by human beings who possess only partial and time-limited knowledge. There may be people with whose religious views we profoundly disagree. But it is not our right to exercise a role which belongs ultimately to Christ alone.

Hubmaier was also convinced that torture and cruel punishment were entirely contrary to the spirit of Jesus: "For Christ did not come to butcher, destroy and to burn." "To burn heretics is in appearance to profess Christ but in reality to deny him." "It is clear to everyone, even the blind, that a law to burn heretics is an invention of the devil." Hubmaier found it inconceivable that those who owned the name of Jesus could justify torturing human beings or burning them alive. Insightfully he observed, "A Turk or heretic is not convinced by our act, either with the sword or with fire, but only with patience and with prayer."

Hubmaier ended his tract with words that have ever since been identified with his name: "Truth is immortal."[21]

Henry Vedder, to whom we are indebted for making available the writings of Hubmaier, made his own commentary on this insight:

"The old zeal for persecuting still survives, and often breaks out in utterly unconscious manifestations in the midst of every religious body. We do not believe that the ark of God is safe unless our hand occasionally steadies it. We have no real confidence at bottom in the ability of the truth to conquer in a fair field, and are impelled from time to time to lend our invaluable aid – always of course on the side of right and truth and justice."[22]

Anabaptism was persecuted out of existence in some European countries. Thousands were put to death for refusing to accept the imposed religious settlement of the land, be it a Protestant or a Catholic settlement. Anabaptists were considered a destabilising force, undermining the unity of the monolithic Church. Cases of Anabaptist activity in mid sixteenth century England have also been found, albeit on a much smaller scale.[23] Often those found guilty faced the same grizzly fate as their Continental counterparts. Intriguingly, however, religious dissent in England was to take a different form. The almost complete dominance of Calvinism amongst English Protestants from the 1550s onwards was to drastically alter the debates within the English Church. Arguments over the nature of the Church and the nature of the Reformation were to take place and to be no less heated than on the Continent. But they took place within a markedly different context and with a very different premise about what the true Church of Christ should look like.

Footnotes

1. G.H.Williams 'The Radical Reformation' p.129 gives his name as Hippolytus (Bolt) Eberli. W.R.Estep 'The Anabaptist Story' p.22 gives him the name Eberli Bolt.
2. 'The Spiritual Resurrection' (1536) found in 'The Complete Writings of Menno Simons' ed. J.C.Wenger p.55
3. 'The New Birth' (1537) in 'Complete Writings' p.96-97
4. 'The New Birth' in 'Complete Writings' p.96
5. 'A Kind Admonition on Church Discipline' (1541) in 'Complete Writings' p.409
6. 'A Kind Admonition' in 'Complete Writings' p.413
7. The full text of this 'Confession of Faith' is printed in 'The Writings of Pilgram Marpeck' ed. Klassen and Klaasen p.108ff
8. 'The Writings of Pilgram Marpeck' p.185
9. 'The Writings of Pilgram Marpeck' p.187
10. Letter 2 'Judgment and Decision' in 'The Writings of Pilgram Marpeck' p.325
11. The full text of 'On the Sword' is reproduced in Kessinger Publishing's reproduction of H.C.Vedder's 1905 'Balthasar Hubmaier: The leader of the Anabaptists' p.273ff
12. 'The New Birth' in 'Complete Writings' p.94
13. Walter Klaassen 'Anabaptism: neither Catholic nor Protestant' p.18
14. H.C.Vedder 'Balthasar Hubmaier' p.193
15. H.C.Vedder 'Balthasar Hubmaier' p.197
16. H.C.Vedder 'Balthasar Hubmaier' p.197
17. Article 7 of Hubmaier's statement of beliefs submitted to Ferdinand of Austria in January 1528. The full text is printed in H.C.Vedder 'Balthasar Hubmaier' p.231
18. The Schleitheim Confession of 1527 was a document produced by the Swiss Brethren (probably Michael Sattler). It had Seven Articles dealing with Baptism, the Ban, Breaking of Bread, Separation, Pastors in the Church, the Sword, and the Oath. The full text can be accessed at www.anabaptists.org/history/schleith.html Sattler was burned at the stake on 20th May 1527. An account of his cruel torture and execution is found in W.R.Estep 'The Anabaptist Story' p.47
19. Found in Walter Klaassen 'Anabaptism: neither Catholic nor Protestant' p.53-54
20. The full text of 'Concerning heretics and those who burn them' can be found in H.C.Vedder 'Balthasar Hubmaier' p.84-88
21. H.C.Vedder 'Balthasar Hubmaier' p.88
22. H.C.Vedder 'Balthasar Hubmaier' p.88-89
23. G.H.Williams 'The Radical Reformation' p.778-781. Included in the list of English Anabaptists were Joan Boucher and Henry Hart

CHAPTER 2

PURITANS AND SEPARATISTS

The Elizabethan Religious Settlement was a compromise.[1] The new Queen was well aware of the necessity of returning the nation to Protestantism following its Catholic period under her half sister, Mary. But Elizabeth was far from desiring the implementation of a full blooded Protestant system as urged by many of the exiles now returning from Geneva. Elizabeth was content with a national Church which affirmed her sovereignty. She retained the bishops; and maintained the conservative religious and Catholic practices of her father, Henry VIII. Either through personal taste or an attempt to win over the Catholic sympathisers, Elizabeth wanted a Church that retained many Catholic features while set in a clearly Protestant framework. Such a compromise, however, was bound to leave many people dissatisfied.

For the Protestants of England, Elizabeth was to be "their darling and their despair."[2] While she considered the 1559 Act of Supremacy and Act of Uniformity her final word on the religious settlement of England, many regarded it as provisional.[3] Barrie White is almost certainly correct when he says that for the first half of her reign it was the Queen's will alone that blocked the policies of her more advanced Protestant subjects.[4] Many of the Queen's advisers were of strong Protestant tendencies. Her Parliaments would have readily implemented a more vigorous reforming programme.[5] It was Elizabeth's resistance, and often intervention, that prevented wholesale reformation of the Church.

Puritanism emerged out of this impasse. Puritanism is a slippery term. It can mean a whole variety of things. While it is commonly used to refer to the "hotter sort of Protestants"[6] it is important to remember that there were 'gradations' of Puritanism.[7] Archbishop Grindal, for example, was seen by a number of people as a Puritan (or at least a 'semi-puritan'[8]), and yet undeniably he dealt harshly with Puritans! There were Puritans who were quite happy with the structure of the

15

Elizabethan Church with its bishops and its Prayer Book. They merely looked for certain flexibility regarding the wearing (or not wearing) of clerical vestments, and the freedom to omit those parts of the Prayer Book they didn't like! But there were other Puritans who wanted nothing less than the overthrow of episcopacy and the establishment of a Presbyterian form of national Church. Chief among these Presbyterians was Thomas Cartwright who was dismissed as Lady Margaret Professor of Divinity at Cambridge following a series of sermons he gave at the University in 1570 advocating Presbyterianism as the pattern of the true primitive Church. Cartwright was compelled to flee the country, but over the next thirty years both in and out of the country, and in and out of prison, he was to promote the Presbyterian model of Church government to an ever widening circle of adherents.

The one thing all these 'Puritans' had in common was their belief that the Church of England as established in 1559 was 'but halfly reformed'.[9] John Knox regarded the Anglican via media as a "mingle-mangle."[10]

Technically, talk of a Puritan Movement only begins with Archbishop Parker's 'Advertisements' of 1566.[11] Prior to that most of those eager for reform were willing to believe that Elizabeth would eventually introduce the changes that were required. Matthew Parker became Elizabeth's first Archbishop in 1559. He ideally suited Elizabeth's mindset having received his Episcopal ordination under Queen Mary and therefore being acceptable to the more conservative leaning of her countrymen. In 1566 the Archbishop, encouraged by the Queen, issued a series of 'Advertisements' or directives which compelled clergy to wear the vestments prescribed in the revised Book of Common Prayer. Hitherto there had been a degree of tolerance shown to clergy who had scruples about wearing clothing which they regarded as vestiges of Roman Catholicism. But in 1566 the Queen and her Archbishop decided that conformity to the rules was required, and Parker ordered the bishops to impose the strict letter of the law. Those clergy who refused to wear the prescribed robes of office were liable for suspension or deprivation.

For many of the bishops themselves this was an unpalatable duty. Most had been exiles in Geneva during Queen Mary's reign and had imbibed the 'sweet nectar' of a Reformed Church from Calvin and his successors. Several of the bishops had only accepted preferment in an Episcopal Church with great reluctance.[12] Ronald Marchant helpfully points to the indifference of successive Archbishops of York (including Grindal) to enforcement of clerical dress codes and adherence to the strict letter of the Prayer Book.[13]

Parker's 'Advertisements' did not prevent individual bishops from implementing the rules at their own discretion. But what it did do was to signal to the country the mind of the Queen, and end any illusion people might have had regarding the reforming tendencies of the monarch.

It would be a mistake to see Puritans as simply against things. In truth Puritans were united in a desire to see a godly nation and a godly Church. To this end they were dismayed by the many ignorant and unlearned clergy who held office in parishes up and down the country. They spoke out frequently, and petitioned the Queen, about the problem of absentee clergy, or clergy who held more than one benefice. Puritanism was also far from being simply a clerical movement. It reflected the mind of very many lay people in England.[14]

To counteract the woeful lack of preaching and teaching that took place in many parishes, and the lack of basic Christian instruction for people brought up solely on a diet of Prayer Book ritual, a whole system of Puritan 'lectureships' were established. These created regular preachers in parishes to supplement what little teaching might already exist. But in addition to these lectureships there also emerged what became known as 'Prophesyings', a Genevan import, which were expositions of scriptural and doctrinal passages designed to educate, instruct and promote the Reformed position. Many of these were held in public and served to instruct laymen, ground people in doctrine and prepare men for the Christian ministry. Collinson sees them as being important for 'indoctrination' and a 'public vindication of the Protestant gospel.'[15]

The Prophesyings were in part an attempt to increase the spiritual understanding and knowledge in the country. Puritans regarded them as essential to the correction of sinners and edification of the saints. But the Queen grew suspicious of them after reports reached her that they were being used as platforms by religious extremists.[16]

Acrhbishop Parker died in 1575, and Edmund Grindal, who had served successively as Bishop of London and then Archbishop of York, replaced him. Grindal's reforming credentials were such as to encourage Puritans. One of the first tasks the Queen asked of Grindal, however, was the suppression of the Prophesyings. The Archbishop refused. And in a letter which Collinson describes as 'tactless' he not only justified the practice but effectively told the Queen she should not interfere in religious matters.[17] The Queen promptly suspended her Archbishop (1577) and he was left sidelined and ineffectual until his death in 1583.

By this time even the most optimistic of Puritans could see that the Queen was unlikely to implement any significant religious changes. Throughout the 1570s a series of conservative episcopal appointments were made, including Edmund Freke to Norwich in 1575, Aylmer to London in 1576, and Whitgift to Worcester in 1577. The power vacuum created by an Archbishop effectively under house arrest was filled by those who shared the Queen's sentiments. Chief among these was John Whitgift.

Whitgift was clearly the dominant ecclesiastical figure in the 1581 Parliament, and few were under any illusion that he was heir apparent.[18] Once Grindal had died, John Whitgift was sworn in as the next Archbishop of Canterbury, and for the next twenty years was to exercise "almost absolute power with despotic severity."[19] Stuart Babbage refers to the "coercive policy"[20] of Whitgift and his able lieutenant, Richard Bancroft, who served in a variety of ecclesiastical roles in the capital until his appointment as Bishop of London in 1597. A measure of Whitgift's intention to establish order and conformity upon the Church was the imposition in 1583 of Three Articles on all those exercising any ecclesiastical office. One of those articles was the requirement to use the prescribed formularies of the Book of Common

Prayer and no others. In the ensuing melee clergy were suspended, others deprived of office, and Archbishop and Privy Council were bombarded by petitions from aggrieved clergy and parishioners. It was only Burghley's intervention that eventually persuaded the Archbishop to grant concessions to those racked with troubled consciences. Collinson believes that such was the level of opposition to the measures that had Parliament been meeting in 1583 when the protests were at their height we probably would not have any bishops or a Church of England today.[21] In 1586 legislation was passed to restrict and control the publication of literature, with all material requiring the approval of either Whitgift or the Bishop of London.

Separatism had its origins in such a climate. The essential difference between Puritanism and Separatism is that the Puritan looked for the reform of the Established Church whereas the Separatist concluded that the Church of England was beyond reform.

A Plumbers' Hall Congregation in London has been traced as early as 1567.[22] It regarded itself as separate from the Church of England, administering its own sacraments, although its members were still part of the official Church. A more thorough going Separatist community was established again in London by Richard Fitz from 1567 – 71. Documents from that community indicate their conviction to purge all remnants of Romanist practice from the Church of England, their foundational text being 2 Corinthians 6: 17 &18 "Come out from among them, and separate yourselves from them."[23] However, as Stuart Burrage writes, "The first Englishman of strong intellectual gifts to win distinction as a preacher of Separatism and as the bold author of works which directly encouraged separation from the Church of England was Robert Browne."[24]

Robert Browne graduated from Corpus Christi, Cambridge in 1572. He was already possessed of advanced Puritan views regarding the true nature of the Church. In 1579 Bancroft removed his preaching licence and so Browne left for Norwich where he had heard there were people of independent religious beliefs. Burrage believes it was not until the Spring of 1581 that his congregation, numbering perhaps no more than 40 people, formally separated themselves from the Established

Church.[25] Arrested and imprisoned a couple of times in 1581 Browne's congregation eventually removed to Middleburg on the continent in January 1582. It was there that Browne set to writing down his theories of separation, most famously in 'A Treatise of reformation without tarrying for anie." Browne envisaged a Church without Archbishops, Deans or Canons; where the people and not the officers constituted the Church; where Elders were appointed by the congregation and where Elders ordained the Pastor.[26]

Crucially, and Browne's unique contribution to Separatist ideology, was his concept of the covenanted community:[27]that a true Church is determined by a mutual covenant between its members pledging commitment to God and to one another. Pivotal to this covenant was the implementation of discipline. The Church of England was not a true Church because Christ did not reign; for to reign was to discipline. Browne advocated a form of dual separation:[28]that while it was essential for Christians to separate from the godless and form a visible and pure Church, it was also necessary to exercise discipline within that Church whereby faltering and wayward church members could be corrected and if need be expelled. This classic formulation became the hallmark of Separatist communities and for the next forty years all such congregations were given the label 'Brownist.' Robert Browne's ecclesiology was the first known sustained attempt by an English Separatist to produce a consistent doctrine of the Church.[29]

The later stages of Browne's career are extremely sad and tinged with a certain amount of irony. The Middleburg congregation "seems to have been a veritable hornets' nest."[30] Browne was excommunicated by his own congregation after a prolonged dispute, and made his way in 1583 to Scotland. He was imprisoned and, after an abortive attempt to settle once more in Middleburg, he returned to England where he eventually renounced all his Separatist convictions and became a conforming member of the Church of England, spending the last forty years of his life as the vicar of Achurch-cum-Thorpe in Peterborough until his death in 1633.[31]

The development of London Separatism can be seen through the careers of John Greenwood and Henry Barrow. While holding views very similar to Browne, Barrie White does not believe there was any causal link, and that their ideas developed independently.[32]

Greenwood had trained at Corpus Christi, Cambridge from 1578-1581. He was ordained and served in Norfolk until he was deprived of office in 1585 for his refusal to use the Book of Common Prayer.[33] On October 8th 1587 he and 22 other Separatists were arrested and imprisoned for holding an illegal conventicle. On November 19th 1587 Henry Barrow, a graduate of Clare College, Cambridge and Gray's Inn, was arrested when he went to consult with Greenwood in the Clink prison. For the next six years the men were to suffer the indignity of London prisons, but this in no way curtailed their literary campaign. During those years Greenwood, and particularly Barrow, produced a wealth of Separatist literature which became foundational in establishing the Separatist position. Barrow's 'A Plaine Refutation' highlighted the four main areas of contention with the Church of England: a false worship; a false membership; a false ministry; and a false government.[34] It was impossible to remain in membership of such a Church, he maintained, and it was incumbent upon all right thinking people to separate themselves from the Church of England.

Barrow and Greenwood made it plain that in matters of religion it was more important to obey God than man. It was this which eventually became interpreted as seditious and led to their conviction for treason. They were hanged on 6th April 1593. Their Separatist colleague, John Penry, was also hanged seven weeks later.

The clandestine London Separatist congregation had continued to survive despite the continued imprisonment of their leaders. In September 1592 they chose a new leader, Francis Johnson. Johnson had been a tutor at Christ's College, Cambridge where his Puritan views and stated preference for Presbyterianism had led to his imprisonment and subsequent dismissal from the University in 1589. He moved to Middleburg where he accepted the position as chaplain to the Presbyterian "Church of Merchant Adventurers."[35] In 1591 he came across Barrow's 'Plain Refutation' with its clear Separatist position. Persuaded by the arguments, Johnson returned to London to confer with Barrow and Greenwood and in due time joined and then led the secret conventicle. In December 1592 Johnson was himself imprisoned for four years. The London Separatist Church took the decision that it was impossible to survive in such a climate of persecution and made the decision to remove to Amsterdam. On his release from prison Francis Johnson joined the now exiled congregation and resumed his leadership. As the oldest of the English exiled communities in Amsterdam they acquired the title of 'The Ancient Church.' Central to Johnson's understanding of the visible Church was his concept of the covenant which was to feature in all Separatist thinking for the next generation.[36]

Separatist theory and practice took shape in the 1580s and 1590s but it remained only at the margins of that wider Puritan Movement. Presbyterian ideology was as intolerant of Separatism as was the Established Church. Both regarded attempts to fragment the unity and uniformity of the Church as dangerous. But Presbyterian rhetoric was directed chiefly at the Church of England. Alongside the more measured literary contributions of Thomas Cartwright there were more vitriolic assaults on Anglicanism by John Field ("The Lenin of Elizabethan Puritanism")[37] and Thomas Wilcox. Their 'Admonition to the Parliament' in 1572 had adopted the strongest possible language, describing the Prayer Book as "that Popish dunghill" and insisting that the Bishops and Archbishops were "drawn out of the Pope's shop."[38] Perhaps the most caustic of all the writings of the Puritan press were those of the pseudonymous Martin Marprelate, the butt of whose humour was directed at individual bishops such as Aylmer, Cooper and Whitgift. Although no-one ever claimed responsibility for this scurrilous and satirical literature, Collinson suggested that John Field had produced some of the material. Field died in 1588 just before the Marprelate tracts were emerging, but a reservoir of his satirical writings could certainly have survived his death.[39]

If Puritan, Presbyterian and Separatist writing, protesting and thinking emerged out of the unwillingness of the centre to make changes to the Religious Settlement, then the impact of that writing and protesting was to make the centre even less inclined to reform. As part of the government reaction to Marprelate there was a general clampdown on Puritan ministers, nine of whom were arrested including Cartwright.

They were accused of being members of Presbyterian Classis meetings, subscribing to the Presbyterian Book of Discipline, and subverting the Queen's authority. In what became a national cause celebre the nine were tried by Church Commissioners in 1590 and then sent to appear before the Star Chamber.[40]

Much of the venom was removed from the campaign against the nine ministers with the death of the Lord Chancellor, Christopher Hatton, in November 1591. There was no real evidence to convict the men, and, but for Whitgift's personal animus, they might have been released. Eventually, the case against them fell apart and a stalemate was reached. In 1595 Cartwright left prison for Guernsey, one of the few places in the British Isles which had seriously embarked upon a full blown Presbyterian experiment.

In 1593 Whitgift was responsible for turning a Parliamentary Bill aimed at Catholic recusants into an Act that dealt with Protestant sectaries.[41] The "Act for the punishment of persons obstinately refusing to come to Church" threatened a jail sentence for any person over the age of sixteen who either refused to attend their Parish Church or was found at any alternative religious gathering. Failure to conform within three months would result in perpetual banishment from the country on pain of death should the felon refuse to leave or return without permission. It was this statute that was used later to harass the Lincolnshire and Nottinghamshire Separatists under King James.

The hope of wholesale reformation of the Church under Queen Elizabeth had completely vanished by the late 1580s. It was more than apparent that no reforms were to be allowed. But for most the idea of abandoning the vision of a national and united Church established on Reformed lines was not one they wished to contemplate. The Queen was getting old. She had no children. And the heir to the throne of England was James VI of Scotland who presided over a Presbyterian Church. Better to wait for the new King than risk futile gestures that alienated the current monarch.[42]It was, therefore, with a sense of biding one's time that the Puritans in Parliament and in the country waited with anticipation the arrival of their new King, an event that was delayed until 1603 through Elizabeth's surprising longevity.

Such was the hope invested in the new King that in August 1603 John Robinson delivered a sermon to his Norwich congregation based on the text from Psalm 118:24 "This is the day that the Lord has made." Robinson called upon his congregation to give thanks to God "for sending him [King James] to reign over us."[43]

The Puritan plans for the new reign were being hatched even as King James made his leisurely jaunt down through England in 1603. In April he was presented with a Millenary Petition, a moderate set of Puritan proposals which would have corrected many of the abuses in the existing ecclesiastical structure and would have gone a considerable way to winning over the majority of Puritans in the country.[44] James acquiesced in the request for a conference to debate some of the Puritan proposals, a decision which considerably encouraged the Puritans even as it dismayed his ageing Archbishop.[45] The conference should have taken place in November 1603 but had to be postponed until the January, and relocated 15 miles outside London to Hampton Court, because of an outbreak of plague in the capital.[46]

The Puritans were ambushed at the Hampton Court Conference. Having been caught on the hop by the King's impulsive decision to agree to the conference, Whitgift and Bancroft had time to regain the initiative. The conference was packed in favour of the Established Church. Only four chosen Puritans (Reynolds, Chaderton, Knewstubs and Sparke) were allowed to contend with an Archbishop, eight Bishops, five Deans, two other clergymen, and a King who was predisposed to give no truck to their arguments. For three days the conference struggled on amidst monarchical tempests as the King expounded the deficiencies of the Presbyterian democracy he had experienced in Scotland. It ended with King James providing a personal and passionate defence of episcopacy, and insisting he would make the Puritans conform or "harry them out of the land."[47]

Within a month of the conference, Archbishop Whitgift had died. His chosen successor, Richard Bancroft, lost no time in capitalising on the advantages gained through the Hampton Court coup. As Parliament met in 1604 then so too did the Canterbury Convocation. Emerging from often vigorous debate within Convocation,[48]Bancroft was instrumental in the passage of 141 Canons which were to define and clarify the Church's position on liturgical and administrative practice. They enshrined in ecclesiastical law the Book of Common Prayer with those practices, such as the signing of the cross at baptism, which the Puritans had wished to see left as matters of conscience. And they established a series of penalties for malefactors that were the source of numerous suspensions and deprivations from ecclesiastical office over the next couple of years, and which were to do more for the cause of English Separatism than any other action taken at this time.[49]

W.K.Jordan stated back in 1936 that King James' handling of the Puritans was politically inept. He managed to alienate a body of goodwill at the outset of his reign that was to turn into fervent opposition.[50] Stuart Babbage made a similar assessment of Richard Bancroft: that while he managed to suppress the Puritan challenge, "the conflict was only postponed and not concluded."[51] The seeds of the English Civil War were already being sewn.

Footnotes

1. Patrick Collinson 'Elizabethan Puritan Movement' (EPM) p.35. It was both a political compromise and a religious compromise. The final form of the 1559 Prayer Book was also a work of compromise (p.33) between conservative and radical elements.
2. Barrie White 'English Separatist Tradition' (EST) p.20
3. Collinson EPM p.35
4. Barrie White EST p.21
5. This is a point which Collinson EPM makes throughout his book. Referring to the House of Commons he says, "In this moderate sense the main body of the House was solidly Puritan in its sympathies."p.315. Walter Burgess 'Smyth, Helwys' was to make a similar point: Queen Elizabeth "was always less Protestant than her Parliaments and less a Reformer than the leading members of her Council." p.14
6. Collinson EPM p.27
7. Collinson EPM p.27
8. Collinson 'Archbishop Grindal' p.187
9. Collinson EPM p.29
10. Collinson EPM p.45
11. David Beale 'The Mayflower Pilgrims' p.7
12. Collinson EPM p.46ff

13. Marchant 'Puritans and the Church Courts in the Diocese of York': at the time of the Advertisements, Archbishop Thomas Young did prosecute a number of prominent clergy for their refusal to conform (p.15-16) but this was not typical. More typical was the tolerance of Archbishop Matthew Hutton (1595-1606) and Toby Matthew (1606-1628) towards the Puritan cause. Such was the tolerance of the Archdeacon of Nottingham, John Lowth, that through him "Puritanism established its first hold in the county." p.132

14. Collinson EPM p.51ff

15. Collinson EPM p.177

16. Collinson EPM p.193

17. Collinson EPM p.196

18. Collinson EPM p.205-206

19. David Beale 'Mayflower Pilgrims' p.10

20. Stuart Babbage 'Puritanism and Richard Bancroft' p.38

21. Collinson EPM p.272

22. Jason Lee 'Theology of John Smyth' p.7

23. Barrie White EST p.29-30

24. Burrage 'Early English Dissenters'(EED) p.94

25. Burrage EED p.97

26. Burrage EED p.101ff

27. Barrie White EST p.53ff

28. Barrie White EST p.57-58

29. Barrie White EST p.66. Champlin Burrage (EED p.101ff) says that Browne never saw separation from the Church of England as permanent or as an end in itself. It was only until such time as that Church had reformed itself.

30. Burrage EED p.111

31. David Beale 'Mayflower Pilgrims' p.12

32. Barrie White EST p.72

33. David Beale 'Mayflower Pilgrims' p.13

34. David Beale 'Mayflower Pilgrims' p.14

35. David Beale 'Mayflower Pilgrims' p.14

36. Barrie White EST p.113. He also mentions the key role 'covenant' played in the writing and thinking of Henry Ainsworth whose devotional work 'The Communion of Saints' was published in 1607.

37. Collinson 'Archbishop Grindal' p.169

38. Collinson EPM p.119-120

39. Collinson EPM p.394. Barrie White EST p.89 mentions that John Penry was another strong candidate for Marprelate. Wikipedia acknowledges Penry as the printer of the tracts but believes the author was Job Throckmorton MP. The full text of these documents can be found online at www.anglicanlibrary.org/marprelate In the first of the tracts, 'The epistle' (October 1588) the bishops are castigated as "pettie Antichrists, pettie popes, proud prelates, intolerable withstanders of reformation, enemies of the gospel, and most covetous wretched priests."

40. Collinson EPM p.409ff gives the details

41. Collinson EPM p.431

42. Burgess 'Smyth, Helwys' p.23
43. Jeremy Bangs 'The Pilgrims, Leiden and the early years of Plymouth Plantation' p.9
44. W.K.Jordan 'Development of Religious Toleration in England' vol.2 p.18 calls the Millenary Petition "reasonable and minor changes in the ritual and discipline of the Church of England." David Beale 'Mayflower Pilgrims' p.19 provides a list of these 'moderate' proposals. They included:
    - That the requirement of the signing of the cross at baptism be discontinued
    - That the requirement of wearing the cap and surplice be discontinued
    - That a sermon should accompany communion
    - Terms such as 'priest' and 'absolution' be discontinued
    - That the Lord's Day be kept but not other holy days
    - That the reading of the Apocrypha be not required
    - That ministers who are unable to preach should be charitably removed
    - That non-residence be forbidden
    - That the lawfulness of ministers' marriages be recognised
45. Stuart Babbage 'Puritanism and Richard Bancroft' Chapter 2
46. Jeremy Bangs 'The Pilgrims, Leiden' p.10
47. David Beale 'Mayflower Pilgrims' p.21. Beale also makes the point that Dr Reynolds did persuade the King at Hampton Court to agree to a new translation of the Bible. It was this decision that was to lead to the King James (Authorised) version of 1611.
48. Stuart Babbage 'Puritanism and Richard Bancroft' Chapter 3
49. Stuart Babbage 'Puritanism and Richard Bancroft' says that the idea of 300 clergy deprived of office as a result of the enforcement of the Canons is probably exaggerated. He believes there were 90 at most. (p.217): "Only the most stubborn and intransigent were actually deprived" p.218. Moreover "if the proportion in the dioceses of London and Lincoln is typical, about one fifth of those who were deprived later conformed." p.217. Even so, it was that core of deprived clergy who became the mainstay of English Separatism. (See Coggins 'John Smyth's Congregation' Chapter 2).
50. W.K.Jordan 'Development of Religious Toleration in England' vol.2 p.20: "The Puritan group was still moderate; it was still devoted to the communion of the Church of England; and the accession of James found it in a temper which might have been utilized by an abler ruler in order to effect a lasting compromise .... But James chose immediately to drive Puritanism into a state of dull resentment which was to grow into flaming opposition before his life was out."
51. Stuart Babbage 'Puritanism and Richard Bancroft' Conclusion

CHAPTER 3

JOHN SMYTH AND THE PILGRIM FATHERS

John Smyth's date and place of birth are uncertain. He was possibly the fourth son of John Smyth of Sturton le Steeple, Nottinghamshire.[1] In March 1586 he was admitted to Christ's College, Cambridge as a "sizar", that is a student of the lower rank, who received food and instruction at a reduced fee in return for performing duties in Hall.[2] He would also be required to perform personal services to the Master or a Fellow including cleaning boots or dressing hair. And as part of his role he would be expected to waken his tutor, valet him and tidy his chamber in time for Chapel at 5.00am.[3]

While Cambridge had very strong Puritan sympathies, Christ's College appeared to be at the very centre of Puritan influence.[4] A whole series of Puritan and later Separatist leaders emerged from Christ's including Richard Bernard, William Perkins, Arthur Hildersham and George and Francis Johnson. Significantly, Smyth studied under Francis Johnson, the future Separatist pastor, and he took his MA in Midsummer 1593. Smyth became a Fellow of Christ's College in 1594 and was ordained by William Wickham, Bishop of Lincoln about the same time.

Some accounts have Smyth in trouble for his Puritan views as early as 1585-6, being cited before the Vice Chancellor for a sermon he delivered on Sabbath keeping.[5] But this would be far too early for our John Smyth and would appear to be another student of the same name.[6] By 1597, however, John Smyth was in trouble, for his objection to the Anglican Burial Service, the churching of women and the use of the surplice.[7] In 1598 Smyth was obliged to resign his Fellowship of Christ's College upon his marriage.[8]

Smyth could easily have found a parish in which to minister, but he avoided this, being aware of the scrutiny this would engender.[9] Instead, on 27th September 1600 Smyth was elected city lecturer for Lincoln. This was a post which gave significantly more freedom to puritan-minded clergy and was a well known device employed by those eager to exercise ministry but avoid responsibility.[10] It also paid better![11] Two years later, on 2nd September 1602, Smyth was appointed city lecturer for life by the mayor, Edward Dynnys. In fact the appointment was to be short lived. Smyth became a pawn in the game of Lincoln's political elite.[12] Accusations were made about the tone of his remarks about the city fathers in one of his sermons[13] and on 13th October Smyth's predecessor as lecturer, Luddington, was appointed in his place. Smyth appears to have practised as a physician in order to make ends meet.[14]

Smyth remained in Lincoln. He buried a son, Jeruball, and baptised a daughter, Mara, at St Peter's, Gowts.[15] In 1603 he published his first work, a collection of four sermons preached in Lincoln on Psalm 22, which was entitled, 'The Bright Morning Starre." The work betrays all the hallmarks of traditional Calvinist thought. Smyth described himself as "preacher of the citie."

On 23rd March 1603 Archbishop Whitgift gave Smyth permission to preach throughout the province of Canterbury.[16] This included Lincoln. The Bishop of Lincoln objected to this, so on 26th July Whitgift revoked the licence. Smyth had little option but to leave Lincoln and take up residence in Gainsborough. He continued to preach, falling foul of the Archdeacon's visitation on 23rd August 1604 for preaching in that parish "notwithstanding being inhibited by the Lord Bishop of Lincoln."[17]

There is a possibility that during this period Smyth was living and working in North Clifton on the Nottinghamshire border. Ronald Marchant[18] notes that in the enquiry of 1604 the churchwardens of North Clifton specified both their vicar and their schoolmaster, John Smyth, as "painfull preachers." Marchant cites Professor A.C.Wood who suggested that schoolmaster Smyth was later to be Separatist Smyth. Interestingly the Oxford Dictionary of National Biography has Smyth down as the curate of Clifton, and notes that on 5th October 1604, as clerk of Clifton, he was charged at East Retford Quarter Sessions with illegal assembly in a dispute over a benefice.

In spite of the institutional harassment Smyth was receiving because of certain heterodox opinions, the fact remains that he was strenuously trying to stay within the Church of England. In his second work, 'The Paterne of True Prayer' Smyth deliberately set out to counter those who had tried to link him to the Separatists. He defended the practise of using set and written prayers; maintained the efficacy of the Lord's Prayer; and publicly disassociated himself from those like his former tutor, Johnson, who had abandoned the Church of England. Nevertheless, despite Smyth's strenuous efforts to remain within the Established Church it became increasingly apparent that he was being given little room for manoeuvre, and little or no chance of preferment.

In March 1606 Smyth was pressed by some of the parishioners at Gainsborough to read some prayers and expound a little on the Psalms. This was a direct result of the continued absence of the vicar, Jerome Phillips, from his duties. Smyth reluctantly agreed, despite having no licence. Letters of support were sent to the Bishop explaining the reasons for this breach. But instead of being commended for his actions Smyth received a further reprimand. It is likely that this was the final straw for Smyth, the catalyst that forced him into the Separatist camp.[19] Of the signatories to the two letters of support, Gervase Helwys was one, and William Hickman another.[20]

William Hickman had bought Gainsborough Old Hall in 1596.[21]Both his mother, Rose, and father, Anthony, had been staunch Protestants. They had fled to Antwerp in the reign of Queen Mary to escape the reintroduction of Catholicism, and William was brought up in exile. Rose Hickman lived with William in the Old Hall. Another of her sons, Anthony (died 1596), had been in conflict with the ecclesiastical powers at Christ's College, Cambridge. Anthony had been admitted to a Fellowship only after obtaining a waver from the Archbishop exempting him from subscribing to the Articles of Faith.[22]Rose Hickman herself was connected, by her sister's marriage, to John Knox, and a letter from Knox warning her of the corrupt Elizabethan Church structure was a prized family possession.[23]

Though unpopular in the town, the Hickman's position and influence allowed them to display Puritan sympathies with some degree of

31

immunity from ecclesiastical control. As a result they were to provide shelter and hospitality to John Smyth and those like-minded men and women who sought to worship in accordance with their conscience and their understanding of the Christian faith.

It is not exactly clear when meetings at the Old Hall began. Smyth himself[24] indicated that he went through nine months of agonising before deciding to abandon the Church of England. Pivotal to this decision was a meeting which took place in 1606 in Coventry at the home of Sir William and Lady Isabel Bowes.[25] Present at the meeting were clergy who had been deprived of office because of their Puritan viewpoints and outspoken criticism of aspects of Church rituals and practices. These included John Dod, John Barbon, Arthur Hildersham from Ashby de la Zouch, and interestingly, the layman Thomas Helwys. Hildersham had been involved in presenting the Millenary Petition to James I and had a fine Puritan pedigree stretching back to the 1590s.[26] But faced with the Separatist challenge he came to the conclusion that the Church of England was after all a true Church, albeit corrupt, and therefore it was his duty to remain in that Church. Hildersham consequently, though suspended and harassed for his nonconformity, did manage to remain within the establishment.[27]Richard Bernard, vicar of Worksop, reached a similar conclusion despite having seriously dallied with Separatism. Bernard's eventual decision to return to the Anglican fold became the spur to Smyth's book 'Paralleles, Censures and Observations' (1609) in which he accused Bernard of "inconstancy and apostasy."[28]

The Coventry meeting seemed to cement the issues in Smyth's mind. But before he was able to do anything about his new found convictions Smyth became dangerously ill.[29] For several weeks he was nursed back to health by the Helwys' at Broxtowe Hall.

In February 1607 Smyth was again in trouble with the ecclesiastical authorities. He was fined for preaching without licence at Basford, near Helwys' home.[30]But by this time Smyth had already decided to cross the Rubicon. He renounced his ordination at the hands of Bishop Wickham and, with those other dissenting friends who had spiritually journeyed with him, Smyth formally drew up a covenant to form them into a visible Church of the Lord's free people.

The wording of the covenant was preserved by William Bradford. Its character and content are crucial for an appreciation of the subsequent developments in John Smyth's thinking:

"They shook off this yoke of antichristian bondage and as the Lord's free people joined themselves (by a covenant of the Lord) into a Church estate, in the fellowship of the gospel, to walk in all His ways made known, or to be made known unto them, according to their best endeavours, the Lord assisting them."[31]

The Baptist historian, W.T.Whitley, has rightly observed the pioneering nature of this covenant.[32] It set in place the recognition that their views were provisional; their understanding partial; that revelation was so often progressive; and that the Lord may yet have more light and truth to set forth from His word.

The idea of the covenant seems to have been lifted from Francis Johnson[33] who had established a covenant with his community of believers in the 1590s. Biblically Smyth's group found precedent in the Israelites covenanting with God in the time of Asa and in the time of Josiah.[34] But equally they found meaningful the faithful of Nehemiah's time who separated themselves from the people of the land. The Book of Revelation was also drawn upon, which commanded: "Come out of her, my people, that ye be not partakers of her sins and that ye receive not her plagues."(Revelation 19:4) The Church of England, like the Church of Rome before it, was regarded as Babylon, the place from which the Lord's true people must flee. To remain was tantamount to apostasy.

The most likely place where this covenant was drawn up and first used was Gainsborough. Smyth, by 1607, was describing himself as 'Pastor of the Church at Ganesburgh.'[35] But the Separatists were already meeting in different venues, and one of these was at the home of William Brewster in Scrooby.[36]

Puritan clergy had continued to function within the Elizabethan Church. At times their resistance to ecclesiastical fiats brought them into controversy, censure and sometimes suspension, but most managed to remain within the parameters of the Elizabethan settlement. The accession of James I, the outcome of the Hampton Court Conference, and especially the ensuing Canons drawn up by Archbishop Bancroft, significantly changed the climate.[37] The enforcement of the Canons and the vigilance of the new hierarchy resulted in a number of clergy being deprived of their livings. Included among these was Richard Clyfton, vicar of Babworth in Nottinghamshire, who was deprived in 1605.

Clyfton had been vicar of Babworth since 1586. His Puritanism can be ascertained from the fact that in 1591 and 1593 he was summoned before the ecclesiastical courts for not wearing the surplice, for not announcing holy days, and for refusing to use the sign of the cross in baptism.[38] Eventually, in the wake of the Bancroft purge, Clyfton was cited for nonconformity on March 15th 1605, the same day Richard Bernard at Worksop was cited for non-subscription to ecclesiastical Canons.[39] Weeks later, having refused to change their minds, they were both deprived of their parishes.

Driving Clyfton and others from the Church served to bring matters to a head. Hitherto those who shared the Puritan views of Clyfton had been able to travel to hear him preach within the structures of the Church of England. And some, like young William Bradford from Austerfield, had been happy to walk miles to attend Clyfton's services at Babworth. Meetings for further instruction and mutual edification within the parish structure had all the menace of a well run home group! By the same token meetings were held at Gainsborough Old Hall long before the group appointed Smyth as their pastor and formed themselves into a Church. But deprived of position, and desirous of a platform from which to preach, Clyfton looked for clandestine places to meet and one of these was the Old Manor House at Scrooby which was the home of William Brewster.

Brewster entered Peterhouse College, Cambridge in December 1580. He was strongly influenced by reformist teaching and preaching, and in 1583 entered the diplomatic service under the tutelage of Sir William Davison. Davison, himself of Puritan persuasion and with links to the exiled Separatist Church in Holland,[40] embarked on confidential royal business to Holland with Brewster in attendance. This further brought the Nottinghamshire youngster into contact with new religious ideas.

Davison's last piece of patronage for Brewster was to secure for him in 1590 the position of Master of Posts at Scrooby, the position made vacant by the death of Brewster's own father.

William Brewster would have travelled to hear Richard Clyfton and John Smyth preach. When Clyfton was deprived in 1605 he appears to have provided a regular meeting place at Scrooby Manor for the Puritans of the district. And when eventually Smyth came to form a covenanted Separatist Church both Clyfton and Brewster became members.

The precise timescale for all this is difficult to work out. Suggestions that the Separatists were meeting at Gainsborough as early as 1602[41] do not fit well with the known chronology of Smyth's own spiritual journey. Informal gatherings may well have taken place under the Hickmans' protection once Smyth arrived in Gainsborough in 1604. But if he was still agonising about breaking with the Church of England as late as 1606 then there can have been no formal Separatist community until after that point. An early date for the Scrooby Meeting is similarly unlikely given Clyfton's position at Babworth until Spring 1605.

The precise relationship between the Gainsborough and Scrooby groups is also difficult to ascertain. William Bradford was clear that "These people became two distinct bodies or churches, and in regard of distance of place did congregate severally."[42] Bradford also recalled that their numbers were drawn from towns and villages from across Nottinghamshire, Lincolnshire and parts of South Yorkshire. But Bradford wrote at least 30 years after the events, and his understanding of the precise relationship between the Scrooby and Gainsborough groups may have had more to do with their relationship in Holland than in England. More particularly there was only ever one covenant agreed among them which would have inclined to the notion of one Church, meeting in different places.[43]

The division of the Separatists into two groups may have been for safety.[44] It may have been for geographical reasons.[45] But it may also have been the result of the different personalities that were emerging.[46] Because, as well as Clyfton and Brewster as potential rivals to Smyth, a further character came on the scene late in the day[47] who was to have a huge impact on events: this was John Robinson.

John Robinson was born in 1575 at Sturton le Steeple, between Scrooby and Gainsborough. Intriguingly it was the same village that Smyth himself may have hailed from. Robinson went to Corpus Christi College, Cambridge in 1592. He excelled in theological study and became a Fellow in 1597. Like Smyth he had to resign his Fellowship following his marriage (to Bridget White, also of Sturton le Steeple). Robinson was ordained. His first parish was in Mundham, Norfolk. He was suspended from this position because of his outspoken sermons. He moved to Norwich where he became city lecturer, but where hostility to his ideas forced him to leave the area and return to his home village. It was while in this vicinity that he would have encountered the ministries of both Smyth and Clyfton. And it would appear that he found Smyth already so well established that he decided it was more appropriate for him to support the newer cause at Scrooby.[48]

In some versions of the story, Robinson became the Teacher at Scrooby, Brewster the Elder, and Clyfton the Pastor,[49] thus completing the pattern of Church organisation laid out in 1Corinthians 12:28. But this may be a neat separation of roles that may not have been anything like as clear cut at the time.

John Robinson was to play a crucial role in the development of the Separatist cause once they had made the move to Holland. The Pilgrim Fathers who settled in America in 1620 all came from Robinson's Church in Leiden. They included a core (Brewster and Bradford for example) who originated in the Scrooby congregation. But before those

36

events can be relayed an assessment is needed of one of the other chief protagonists in this venture who is so often overlooked. To him we shall turn in the next chapter.

A speculation

Patrick Collinson[50] paints a fascinating picture of Cambridge life: "We are here at the great age of the tutors .... A tutor negotiated directly with his pupil's family to secure his fees as well as to fulfil his moral responsibilities. Puritan parents and dons sought each other out and together conspired for the godly advancement of their charges." If this is an accurate picture then is it possible that Smyth's choice of Christ's College was made because of its avowed Puritanism. Did Smyth's family already have a strong inclination towards Puritanism? And when it is remarked that Francis Johnson was Smyth's tutor does that perhaps suggest not a chance happening but a predetermined arrangement? (To counter that viewpoint William Haller, in his 1938 'Rise of Puritanism' p.183, maintained that Smyth was converted to the Puritan faith while at Christ's College).

If it is true that both John Robinson (born ca. 1575) and John Smyth (born ca. 1571)[51] were from the tiny village of Sturton le Steeple (a remarkable coincidence!) would it not only indicate a strong Puritan presence in that community,[52] but strongly suggest that Smyth and Robinson knew each other from their childhood days. Did connections from much earlier times play a part in reconnecting these men in 1607?

Footnotes

1. Barrie White, in a 'Biographical Dictionary of British Radicals in the 17th Century' ed. Greaves and Zeller 1984. Smyth's birth in Sturton le Steeple is also given in the new Oxford Dictionary of National Biography. Both Stephen Wright 'Early English Baptists' p.13 and Jason Lee 'The Theology of John Smyth' p.41 repeat this.
2. Burgess 'John Smith, Thomas Helwys and the first Baptist Church in England' 1911 p.28
3. W.T.Whitley 'The Works of John Smyth': biographical section p.xix
4. Jason Lee 'The Theology of John Smyth' p.42. Patrick Collinson 'The Elizabethan Puritan Movement' (EPM) p.125 refers to Laurence Chaderton,

the President of Christ's in 1560s and 1570s, as "the pope of Cambridge puritanism [who] ... made Christ's a puritan seminary in all but name."

5. E. Catherine Anwyl 'John Smyth the Se-Baptist' 1991

6. The Biographical Register of Christ's College 1505 – 1905 compiled by John Peile 1910

7. Barrie White 'The English Separatist Tradition' (EST) p.116

8. Burgess 'Smith, Helwys and the first Baptist Church' p.47

9. A.C.Underwood 'A History of the English Baptists' p.34

10. Collinson EPM p.50: "The great age of puritan lectureships, salaried preaching appointments in parish churches which offered a reasonable livelihood and freedom from the restraint of the Prayer Book."

11. Whitley 'Works' p.xli – Smyth's stipend as lecturer of Lincoln was £40 a year plus £3.6.8 for rent and permission to keep three cows on the common! Whitley points out that this stipend was 8 times as much as the vicar of Sturton le Steeple received and 10 times as much Hugh Bromhead received as vicar of North Wheatley.

12. W.R. Estep 'The Anabaptist Story' p.217 – 218

13. E. Catherine Anwyl 'John Smyth' says Smyth was deposed for his "strange doctrines" according to the Bishop of Lincoln's Commission in January 1603

14. A.C.Underwood 'History' p.34

15. Whitley 'Works' p.xlv: Whitley notes that the Smyths called their daughter Mara (Hebrew: 'bitter') rather than Mary after her mother "as if her parents felt that the Lord was dealing bitterly with them."

16. Jason Lee 'Theology' p.45

17. Barrie White EST p.120

18. Marchant 'Puritans and Church Courts 1560 -1642' p.150

19. W.R. Estep 'The Anabaptist Story' p.218

20. E. Catherine Anwyl 'John Smyth'

21. Jennifer Vernon 'Gainsborough Old Hall and the Mayflower Pilgrim Story'

22. Sue Allan 'Lady Rose Hickman: her life and family' p.24

23. Sue Allan 'Tudor Rose' p.142-143

24. 'Paralleles, Censures and Observations' (1609) p.534 in Whitley: 'Works of John Smyth'

25. Whitley 'Works' p.lvii says that Sir William Bowes had offered bail for Francis Johnson when he was imprisoned in Cambridge. The conference was all night long (p.lviii). In his later article ('Thomas Helwys of Grays Inn' BQ vol vii) Whitley says that Sir William arranged the conference at his Coventry home and Helwys brought Smyth and Bernard with him. It would be fair to say that Smyth and Bernard had very different recollections of what happened and what was agreed at that crucial meeting.

26. Collinson EPM p.405 & 428. See also Burgess 'Smyth, Helwys' p.66-68

27. Burgess 'Smyth, Helwys' p.70. Stuart Babbage 'Puritanism and Richard Bancroft' p.185-186 provides a detailed breakdown of Hildersham's later career including his suspensions and persistent nonconformity. In 1616 he was reported for refusing to receive Holy Communion kneeling, and as late as

1630 he was suspended for refusing to wear the surplice. Babbage describes Hildersham as "an impenitent Puritan to the end of his days."

28. Whitley 'Works' p.332. Smyth also says that he and Bernard first embraced the Separatist truth "at Sir W Bowes his house" p.331. Haller 'The Rise of Puritanism' p.137-139 provides a very useful account of Bernard's literary output before and after his move to Somerset in 1613. His works were designed to be spiritually edifying and instructive, and exemplified that strand of Puritan piety that stayed within the Church of England.

29. Smyth 'Paralleles' (Whitley 'Works' p.534) refers to being 'sick almost to death'. In 'The Last Book of John Smyth' (Whitley 'Works' p.759) he refers to the great help he was provided by Helwys when he was sick at Bashforth (Broxtowe): "I was troublesome and chargeable to him."

30. Marchant 'Puritans and Church Courts' p.156

31. William Bradford 'Of Plymouth Plantation' p.8

32. Whitley 'Works' p.lxii

33. Barrie White EST p.122-123. However, Walter Burgess 'Smyth, Helwys' p.85-86 insists that the words of the actual covenant were Smyth's and that this covenant had a broader outlook than Johnson's.

34. Burgess 'Smyth, Helwys' p.82-83

35. 'Paralleles, Censures, Observations' (Whitley 'Works' p.331) which includes a letter written to Mr Richard Bernard, minister of Worksop, by John Smyth 'Pastor of the Church at Ganesburgh'.

36. There are suggestions that the group met in various locations other than Gainsborough Old Hall. Stephen Wright ('Early English Baptists' p.14) suggests that Lady Isabel Bowes home at Walton in Chesterfield was used for 'several local consultations.' And Whitley (BQ vol vii p.247) is fairly sure that one place that was used for worship was Broxtowe Hall.

37. Barrie White EST p.119

38. Jeremy Bangs 'The Pilgrims, Leiden, and the early years of Plymouth Plantation' p.13

39. Marchant 'Puritans and Church Courts' p.149. As well as Bernard and Clyfton, Robert Southworth and Henry Gray were also dealt with in the same way. Marchant points out, however, that for some reason Bernard's living at Worksop was not filled, allowing him to resume his ministry there once he had returned to the fold two years later.

40. Crispin Gill 'The Mayflower remembered' p.24

41. John Brown 'The Pilgrim Fathers of New England' p.83; David Beale 'The Mayflower Pilgrims' p.165

42. William Bradford 'Of Plymouth Plantation' p.8-9

43. Coggins 'John Smyth's Congregation' p.56-61

44. David Beale 'The Mayflower Pilgrims' p.166

45. Crispin Gill 'Mayflower remembered' p.25 suggests that because they had nine miles to walk to Gainsborough it made more sense to make the shorter walk to Scrooby Manor House. James Coggins, however, ('John Smyth's Congregation p.57) points out that several of the Nottinghamshire Separatists appear to have frequented the Gainsborough meeting rather than the Scrooby

one even though Scrooby was nearer, so that "geography alone does not explain the division." Whitley ('Works' p.lxiii – lxiv) makes the astute point that locations for meeting were in part determined by proximity to county borders in order to evade detection by the constables. Worksop (Richard Bernard's territory) never seems to have been considered as a location for meeting because it was too far away.

46. Champlin Burrage 'The Early English Dissenters' p.231 draws attention to Richard Clyfton's 'The plea for infants' (1610) which refers to differences between him and Smyth over excommunication while they were still in England. Stephen Wright 'The Early English Baptists' p.22 helpfully points out that Robinson was also at odds with Smyth prior to their departure for Holland. The issue seems to have been the harsh stance Smyth was taking on refusing to have any fellowship with people unless they also belonged to a Separatist community.

47. Stephen Wright 'Early English Baptists' p.20 notes that Robinson was still in Norwich as late as January 1607 when baptising his daughter, Bridget, at St Peter, Hungate.

48. Vernon Heaton 'The Mayflower' p.34: "John Robinson soon learned that the Gainsborough group of Separatists preferred the Bible-thumping of John Smith to his own more reasoned and less inflammatory teachings and, with some reluctance, gradually came to adopt the Scrooby group for his full time ministrations." Whitley ('Works' p.lxviii) says that Robinson took the role that had effectively been set aside for Bernard until the latter returned to the Church of England. Bishop Joseph Hall, a contemporary and correspondent, remarked that Robinson was very much the junior to Smyth.

49. Edmund Jessup 'The Mayflower Story' p.7

50. Collinson EPM p.125

51. Venn's 'Alumni Cantabrigienses' (1927) states that Smyth was "under age in 1589" which was the date of his father's will.

52. David Beale 'The Mayflower Pilgrims' p.115 points out that another Separatist (one of the Mayflower passengers), Catherine Carver, was also from Sturton le Steeple.

CHAPTER 4

THOMAS HELWYS AND THE GREAT ESCAPE

John Smyth's life has been well documented for nearly a hundred years. Much of Thomas Helwys' life by contrast is shrouded in mystery. Whole periods of his life – especially the last four years – are lost in the mists of time. And even on the most basic and elementary details of his life there are widely divergent opinions.

Wikipedia follows one tradition which has Helwys born c.1550. It is this tradition that appears in the memorial plaque to Helwys in Bilborough Baptist Church, Nottingham,[1] and the same tradition that is repeated even very recently in the Baptist Quarterly.[2] In fact Thomas Helwys was born c.1575. Walter Burgess[3] has convincingly proved that the Thomas Helwys born in 1550 was in fact uncle to our Thomas who, just to add to the confusion, also had a cousin with the same name!

The Helwys family are recorded in Nottinghamshire from the 14th century. William Helwys of Askham (Thomas's grandfather) died in 1557. Thomas' father, Edmund, inherited lands throughout large parts of Nottinghamshire and Lincolnshire, and in 1585 he sold some of these to take out the lease on Broxtowe Hall near Nottingham.[4] Thomas himself was born at Askham Hall, the family home, near Retford.[5]

Edmund Helwys was a God-fearing man who would have made a profound impression on his children. In 1589, soon after the defeat of the Spanish Armada, Edmund published a book entitled 'A Marvell Deciphered,' an exposition of Revelation Chapter 12, in which 'a woman clothed with the sun' was said to be Queen Elizabeth defeating the Catholic dragon. The following year he drew up his will which is heavily laden with Biblical references. He expressed confidence that "Christ hath delivered us from the curse of the Law in as much as he was made accursed for us" (Galatians 3), and "through this belief I hope with St Paul to be purged from all my sins which I confess are many and most wicked."[6] Edmund Helwys died shortly after his will was drawn up and was buried on 24th October 1590. Tragically his daughter Anne died at the same time and was buried in the same tomb in Bilborough Parish Church.[7]

Ernest Payne, in an address at Bilborough Baptist Church on April 7th 1967, said that Thomas Helwys "in his youth" became drawn into the fellowship of the early Puritans.[8] That would seem to be a very fair assumption.

Thomas Helwys was sole executor of his father's will. But still not sixteen years old, and, therefore, a minor in the eyes of the law, Helwys' affairs came under the control of his two uncles.[9] It was probably through their influence that Thomas was sent to Gray's Inn in London where he was enrolled on January 29th 1593.

Helwys' time in London coincided with two major religious incidents. Elizabeth's eighth Parliament was called, and, in response to the Commons' petition for freedom of speech, Elizabeth issued a stern reply effectively telling them not to meddle with the religious settlement. Perhaps more significantly was the execution in 1593 of the Separatists Henry Barrow and John Greenwood. It is inconceivable that to a young man already predisposed to Puritan sympathies these events would not have had a profound effect.[10]

After two years in London, Helwys returned to Broxtowe Hall. On December 3rd 1595 he married Joan Ashmore in Bilborough Parish Church, and the two of them settled down to the life associated with a country squire. The couple were to have seven children. The oldest, John, was baptised as an infant in the Parish Church on September 5th 1596.[11] A further son, called Thomas, was baptised at Bilborough on 13th October 1603.[12]

Joan Helwys shared the religious convictions of her husband.[13] Even their marriage ceremony was carried out without many of the Church of England formularies which subsequently brought the legality of their marriage into question.[14] Several commentators have assumed that Broxtowe Hall would have been a meeting place for Puritan clergy,[15] and may even have been a venue for Separatist gatherings.[16] We know from John Smyth's own statements that he was nursed through a very dangerous illness at Broxtowe Hall for which he was enormously grateful to the Helwys'.[17] Smyth and Helwys became close friends,[18] and Thomas and Joan probably became members of Smyth's congregation meeting in Gainsborough Old Hall.[19]

Thomas and Joan Helwys' religious convictions start to become clearer through an examination of Court Records for this period. On May 15th 1606 they were cited for not taking Communion at Bilborough Parish Church. Cited with them were Henry Gibson and Francis Hill. At Basford on 11th April 1608 the pair were again cited for not attending Church. With them were "Mother Cooke" and Thomas Bates described as 'Sojourners' with Helwys, and Helwys' servant whose last name was Pigot.[20]

If it was a tortuous decision for Anglican Clergymen to renounce their ordination and become Separatists then it must have been equally traumatic for Thomas and Joan Helwys. With land, wealth and position they had much to lose, and Thomas could not have taken the step lightly. Helwys was still noted as attending Basford Parish Church as late as 29th September 1607 (Michaelmas), months after Smyth had made the breach.[21]

William Bradford recalls that the fledgling Separatists were "hunted and persecuted on every side."[22] And while more recent accounts have played down the amount of official or even popular harassment,[23] the fact remains that life was becoming intolerable for the group while ever they refused to conform. In consequence, while the decision to separate from the Church of England was an agonised one, the decision to leave England for the comparative safety of the continent was much easier. Repression had provided them with few alternatives.

The decision to leave appears to have been Smyth's.[24] The choice of destination was clear. Francis Johnson's Ancient Church had already been established in Amsterdam for a generation and was a natural rallying point. Holland provided a safe haven for various religious groups, and William Brewster had himself spent time there in the diplomatic service as a young man. If Smyth provided the vision for the exodus, however, it was Thomas Helwys who was to mastermind the details.[25]

John Robinson, writing in 1614 to counter some of Helwys' harsh criticisms, had to concede that his opponent had been crucial to the whole move to Amsterdam:

"The truth is, it was Mr Helwisse, who above all either guides or others, furthered this passage into strange countries; and if any brought oars he brought sails, as I could show in many particulars, and as all that were acquainted with the manner of our coming over, can witness with me."[26]

Precisely how Helwys furthered their passage isn't clear. There is a possibility that Helwys may have spent part of 1607 making preparations in Amsterdam for the arrival of the Separatists. As a wealthy man he would have had the means and the opportunity to travel without arousing any suspicion. Bishop Joseph Hall indicated that on a visit to the Low Countries at this time he discovered that a "harbinger" from the Clyfton–Smyth group had been out there before him.[27]

W.T.Whitley, in his early writings, was confident that "Helwys was acknowledged as the promoter and capable organiser of the expedition,"[28] "Helwys probably making all the business arrangements."[29] And in his later writings Whitley expanded on this.

Helwys "secured a spacious block of premises on the river Amstel with a courtyard extending to the city ramparts. It belonged to Jan Munter who had used it to bake biscuit ..... The bake-house could be adapted to provide common rooms and family lodgings .... To this refuge, after striking adventures, he brought scores of emigrants from a score of villages by July 1608; and it was destined to be his home for four years."[30]

None of the accounts of the Pilgrim Fathers I have read have made any acknowledgement to Helwys' contribution. It is one of the grievous omissions in that particular narrative.

The time and date of the departure for Holland is still hazy, and subject to widely different opinions. Much of the disagreement centres on the precise relationship between the Scrooby and Gainsborough congregations. Some accounts place all the Separatists in Holland by 1606.[31] Other versions place the arrival of the Gainsborough group in Holland by late 1606, but date the arrival of the Scrooby group as late as 1608.[32] Indeed one scenario dates the emergence of the Scrooby group based on the Old Manor House as the direct consequence of Smyth and the Gainsborough party having abandoned their brethren and departed for Amsterdam.[33]

William Bradford was clear that the Scrooby congregation made two attempts to leave. The first attempt was in 1607. William Brewster resigned his position as Postmaster in September of that year.[34] An English ship was hired to transport perhaps 60 or 70 men, women and children from Boston, Lincolnshire. The captain was a rogue. Having ransacked the group's cargo and robbed them of their possessions he notified the authorities who managed to throw the whole lot of them into prison in Boston.[35] When eventually they were released most were penniless having sold all their possessions in advance of the journey. It was in the Spring of 1608 that the Scrooby congregation made a second attempt.

Hiring this time a Dutch captain to collect them from Immingham, the group decided to split into two in order to avoid capture. The men walked over land while the women travelled by boat down the Trent and the Humber. After their disastrous experience the previous year the men were naturally suspicious, and proceeded onto the ship first. By the time they were convinced of the captain's good intentions and had signalled for the longboat to fetch their women and children an armed raiding party was observed heading for the beach. The Dutch captain, despite all the protestations of the men on board, was forced to depart immediately, leaving the women and children to the fate of the police and the magistrates once again. A disastrous storm greeted the ship once out from the shore. They were at sea for fourteen days before eventually arriving in Amsterdam.[36]

Destitute and reduced to begging the women were eventually shipped abroad to join their menfolk, much to the relief of the civil authorities. Robinson, Clyfton and Brewster had remained behind to ensure everyone did eventually make the journey. They arrived in Amsterdam in August 1608.[37]

While these details appear to be reasonably accurate (they have certainly passed into Pilgrim folklore), the timetable of events is worth re-examination. The Gainsborough group, for example, had arrived in Amsterdam by the Summer of 1608.[38]But they could not have been there long before that. John Smyth was most likely still in England in November 1607.[39] Several others were under arrest or cited to appear before the courts in early 1608.[40] Stephen Wright, therefore, is probably not far wrong when he estimates that "None can have reached Amsterdam before April (1608)."[41]

With such a revised timetable for the Gainsborough group it seems impossible to talk of two separate migrations of the Gainsborough and Scrooby Separatists. Instead, Smyth's adherents came over to Holland "in the same wave of emigration" as Clyfton and Robinson.[42] This tallies with Robinson's own recollection that Helwys (from the Gainsborough group) made possible the emigration of the Scrooby members.[43] Champlin Burrage was certainly of the opinion that "the two companies seem to have reached Amsterdam about the same time."[44]Any divisions between the Separatists came after they arrived in Holland, not before.[45]

Thomas Helwys appears to have organised and funded[46] the whole enterprise. But Helwys was to make still further sacrifices for the cause. By 1610 Broxtowe Hall had been sequestrated by the civil authorities, and King James had leased it out to others.[47]And while Helwys managed to secure the safe passage of so many people to Amsterdam, the one person he was unable to bring over was his wife.

Joan Helwys was in York prison in 1608.[48] It is quite possible that she was convicted and sentenced with Gervase Nevile on 10th November 1607.[49] She certainly appeared in court on the same day as Nevile (22nd March 1608).[50] Nevile, it would seem, was subsequently released, having answered his interrogators in somewhat adequate fashion. He next appears as part of Smyth's congregation in Amsterdam.[51] Joan Helwys ('Elwish'), however, refused to take an oath that was put to her and was remitted to prison (again?) along with John Drewe and Thomas Jessop.[52] Marchant notes that Drewe and Jessop both eventually joined Smyth's church in Amsterdam, and that Joan was released sometime in the Summer.[53]

A second case against her, however, was launched in July 1608.[54] She, along with her husband and several other friends and family members, were accused of being Brownists, and for failing to attend Communion at Basford Parish Church. (In truth Joan could hardly have taken communion at Basford because she had been in York prison!) There was difficulty in apprehending them, and eventually in August, a bond that had been given for Joan's guaranteed appearance in court was ordered forfeit.[55]

Ernest Payne believed that Joan was placed under house arrest in 1607, only being imprisoned in March 1608.[56] Burgess believes that "Joan Elwaies of Basford" completed three months imprisonment after which she was banished.[57] It is the suggestion that Joan was banished that has led some writers to assume she joined her husband in Amsterdam.[58] But in truth, as Burgess pointed out, there are no records of Joan Helwys' presence in Amsterdam and every reason to assume that "she may have found refuge with her own friends or her husband's kindred in London."[59] Thomas Helwys himself, writing in 1611 in Amsterdam, lamented the separation from his family: "Have we not neglected ourselves, our wives, our children and all we had…?"[60]

There is a real mystery why Joan Helwys never managed to join her husband in Amsterdam. If Helwys had secured passage for so many people then it is strange that he couldn't also organise his own family's transport. Did Helwys leave England before Joan's imprisonment in the assumption that his wife and family would be left alone with him out of the way?[61] Marchant observes that the authorities made relatively few arrests but those that were made were of prominent figures intended to set an example.[62] Or did Thomas Helwys leave England after his wife's imprisonment on the understanding that he would set up home for them both in Holland ready for her release?[63] Whichever narrative we adopt the mystery remains why Joan Helwys never made it to Holland. Perhaps the solution to this mystery is to be found in some aspect of the family's life that made travel all but impossible.[64] W.K.Jordan made the simple, but perhaps astute, remark that Joan Helwys "chose to remain in England."[65]

Jason Lee says that the arrest and imprisonment of Joan Helwys and the others was the trigger for the group's decision to leave England.[66]

Alternative suggestions

While Thomas Helwys' status as a wealthy man makes him a prime candidate for the principal funder of the expedition, there are at least a few other suggestions worth making. The pilgrims themselves may well have contributed in part to their own costs, hence their alarm and dismay at being fleeced in Boston and then left destitute at Killingholme. William Brewster would have been a man of some considerable means, and there have been those who have championed Brewster as a chief benefactor.[67] It would also be worth remembering the role played by William Hickman in proceedings. The shelter and protection he afforded the Separatists may well have had a more direct financial element to it.[68] But the suggestion has also been made that John Smyth himself might have helped to underwrite the venture, either through the proceeds of his medical practice or the settlement he received from being dislodged as city lecturer in Lincoln.[69] While these ideas are all possessed of some plausibility the balance of opinion has to be that it was Thomas Helwys who, in Robinson's words " above all other guides or others furthered this passage into strange countries."[70]

Footnotes

1.   Thomas Helwys
c.1550 – c. 1616
Member of the Gainsborough Separatist Church
Companion of John Smyth in Amsterdam
Leader of the first London Baptist Church
Author of the first plea in English for full
Liberty of conscience
Who lived for some years near this spot
At
Broxtowe Hall

An article in the Nottingham Evening Post for March 2nd 1967 says Helwys was born in 1565!

2.   Brian Haymes in BQ vol.42 July 2007: 'On Religious Liberty: re-reading a Short Declaration of the Mystery of Iniquity in London 2005.' I notice that Richard Groves in his edition of 'Mystery of Iniquity' p.xix also has Helwys born in 1550. W.K.Jordan 'The Development of Religious Toleration in England' vol.2 p.274 also has Thomas born in 1550. He notes the anomaly this causes in that Helwys would have been 43 years of age when he was admitted to Gray's Inn!!
3.   Burgess 'Transactions of the Baptist Historical Society' vol.iii 1912/13 p.18ff: 'The Helwys Family.'
4.   Burgess 'Smyth, Helwys and the first Baptist Church' p.112
5.   Article by F.C.Atton, (1962): 'The early days of the Helwys family' in the EMBA Archive, Market Harborough.
6.   Burgess 'Smyth, Helwys' p.111
7.   Burgess 'Smyth, Helwys' p.112
8.   The Baptist Times for April 19th 1967 featured the address in its article: 'Memorial plaque to Thomas Helwys unveiling at Bilborough Baptist Church.' A copy of the article has been preserved in the EMBA Archive in Market Harborough.
9.   J. Glenwood Clayton 'Thomas Helwys: a Baptist Founding Father' in 'Baptist History and Heritage' vol.iii Jan. 1973. Clayton states that Thomas came under the control of his two uncles and two friends, Sir Thomas and Edward Stanhope.
10. Fred Harrison 'The Nottinghamshire Baptists' vol. 1 page 3: "It is likely that during this period Helwys adopted Separatist views and perhaps the martyrdom of Barrow and Greenwood had something to do with it."
11. Burgess 'Transactions of BHS' vol.iii wanted to correct the mistake in his earlier work 'Smyth, Helwys and the first Baptist Church' in which he had incorrectly given the date of John Helwys birth as 1595!
12. Burgess 'Smyth, Helwys' p.115
13. Rev J.T.Crozier 'Some notable women in Baptist history.'

14. Jeremy Bangs 'The Pilgrims, Leiden and the early years of the Plymouth Plantation' p.20. Thomas and Joan were accused of being fornicators in 1596 and 1598 with their irregular marriage still mentioned as late as 1613.
15. Burgess 'Smyth, Helwys' p.114; J.Glenwood Clayton in 'Baptist History and Heritage' vol.viii Jan 1973 'Thomas Helwys: a Baptist Founding Father' p.4
16. Jeremy Bangs 'The Pilgrims, Leiden' p.19
17. 'The Last Book of John Smyth' in Whitley 'Works' p.759
18. Burgess 'Smyth, Helwys' p.115: "Smyth and Helwys were close and intimate friends, and they went heartily together in the way of Separation." Whitley 'Works' p.lvi says that Thomas Helwys, evidently about the same age as Smyth, "soon became his closest friend."
19. Richard Groves in his introduction to the republished edition of 'A Short Declaration of the Mystery of Iniquity' p.xxi. An interesting online article (www.exlibris.org/nonconform/engdis/) suggests that Helwys was Elder at Gainsborough. This might be right. Champlin Burrage 'The Early English Dissenters' (EED) p.236 refers to a letter of Thomas Helwys in the Lambeth Palace Library (MS 709 fol.117) which is dated Sept. 26th 1608. The letter makes clear that Smyth's congregation did not believe in having 'pastors and teachers' but 'pastors only'. It is marked: 'A not(e) sent by Ellwes, one of the elders of the Brownist Church.
20. Jeremy Bangs 'The Pilgrims, Leiden' p.20
21. Stephen Wright 'Early English Baptists' (EEB) p.20-21
22. William Bradford 'Of Plymouth Plantation' p.9
23. Coggins 'John Smyth's Congregation' p.43 believes it inappropriate to talk about 'persecution' of the Separatists. 'Judicial harassment' might be a more accurate description. Stephen Wright EEB p.1-4 is at pains to play down the persecution of the religious dissenters. While the whole tenor of Ronald Marchant's 'Puritans and Church Courts' is to describe the tremendous degree of toleration shown to the Puritans especially under Elizabeth.
24. Whitley 'Works' p.118: "Smyth was the first to conceive a deliberate emigration and to carry it out successfully.... Smyth organised a systematic removal of his whole church at Gainsborough to settle down complete as the same community in another land."
25. Barrie White EST p.125
26. 'Works of John Robinson' vol.3, 'Of Religious Communion' chapter iii, 'Of flight and persecution' p.159
27. 'A common apologie for the Church of England' in Burrage EED p.231
28. Whitley 'Works' p.lxxiv
29. Whitley 'Works' p.lxxvi
30. Whitley BQ vii 1934-5 p.248 James Coggins, however, ('John Smyth's Congregation' p.60-61) does not believe the move into the bake-house happened straight away. He believes it would have been too small for the whole Scrooby-Gainsborough congregation. Coggins believes that Smyth and Helwys' congregation only moved in there AFTER Robinson had taken off a large group to Leiden. This was February 1609.
31. Adam Taylor 'History of the General Baptists' part one p.67

32. Vernon Heaton 'The Mayflower' p.37
33. J.Keith Cheetham 'On the trail of the Pilgrim Fathers' p.26 (book found in the Worksop Library). The same idea can be found in an internet article. It suggests that Clyfton, Brewster, and Robinson all worshipped at Gainsborough with Smyth until Smyth and the Gainsborough core had departed, after which they met at Scrooby Manor.
   See: http://myweb.tiscali.co.uk/sherwoodtimes/scrooby.htm
34. Vernon Heaton 'The Mayflower' p.37
35. Vernon Heaton 'The Mayflower' p.38 based on William Bradford 'Of Plymouth Plantation' p.12
36. William Bradford 'Of Plymouth Plantation' p.13-14
37. Coggins 'John Smyth's Congregation' p.44: Richard Clyfton's family Bible had inscribed the fact that Clyfton, his wife and children, arrived in Amsterdam in August 1608.
38. Transactions of BHS vol.iii 1912/13 "The arrival of Smyth's followers at Amsterdam by July 1608." The author observes that the Amsterdam marriage registers record the marriage of Henry Cullandt of Nottinghamshire and Margaret Grymsdiche of Sutton cum Lound nr. Retford on 5th July 1608. Their banns of marriage had previously been published at Sutton by Richard Clyfton.
39. Coggins 'John Smyth's Congregation' p.39 & 44. This is based on the dating of Richard Bernard's 'Christian Advertisements' to June 1608 and working back 6 or 7 months to the date of Smyth's letter to him. See 'Paralleles, Censures and Observations' Whitley 'Works' p.329. Smyth's letter was sent from England.
40. Stephen Wright EEB p.21
41. Stephen Wright EEB p.21
42. Stephen Wright EEB p.7
43. 'The Works of John Robinson' vol.3 'Of Religious Communion' chapter iii 'Of flight and persecution' p.159
44. Champlin Burrage EED p.232
45. Coggins 'John Smyth's Congregation' p.57-58
46. A.C. Underwood 'A History of the English Baptists' p.34-35: "the funds for the emigration being provided, apparently, by a well to do member of the church, Thomas Helwys of Broxtowe Hall, Nottinghamshire." Ernest Payne 'Thomas Helwys and the first Baptist Church in England' p.6: "Helwys may have financed as well as directed the not inconsiderable venture of getting the company across the sea." The same point is made by James E Tull, 'Shapers of Baptist thought' p.14
47. Stephen Wright EEB p.2 and p.46; Whitley BQ vii 'Thomas Helwys of Grays Inn' p.248 "Broxtowe Hall was seized by the King, who within two years granted the lease to other holders." Walter Burgess 'Transactions of BHS' vol.iii 'The Helwys family' puts a different gloss on this event (p.30). Noting that Broxtowe had passed out of the Helwys' hands he wonders whether this might have been simply because the lease had lapsed, or indeed because Thomas Helwys had sold the lease "to supply his needs in Holland and

further the printing of his books." The calendar of state papers notes that a lease of the manors of Broxtowe in Nottinghamshire and Mapperley in Derbyshire was granted on June 11th 1610 to Andrew Wilson and Lancaster Gibbon.

48. Stephen Wright EEB p.21
49. Marchant 'Puritans and Church Courts' p.160
50. Marchant p.162
51. Marchant p.160
52. Marchant p.162
53. Marchant p.162
54. Marchant p.162
55. Marchant p.163
56. Ernest Payne 'Thomas Helwys and the first Baptist Church in England' p.7
57. Burgess 'Smyth, Helwys' p.116
58. Jeremy Bangs 'The Pilgrims, Leiden' p.20
59. Burgess 'Smyth, Helwys' p.116-117
60. 'Declaration of faith of English people remaining at Amsterdam in Holland.' The quote is found in Coggins 'John Smyth's Congregation' footnote 10 on page 200
61. A.C.Underwood 'A History of the English Baptists' p.46
62. Marchant p.159
63. David Beale 'The Mayflower Pilgrims' p.170
64. Ernest Payne 'Thomas Helwys' p.7 reminds us that the Helwys' had seven children under the age of 12 by 1608. The names of the children are given in an article on Broxtowe Hall in the Nottinghamshire Guardian some time about the 1930s, which has been preserved in the EMBA Archives. John was the oldest (b.1596); Thomas was baptised in 1603; while Gervase, Margaret, Elizabeth, a 2nd Margaret (had the first child by that name died?) and Winifred were all additions to the family. Some of these must have been babies. One or two may not have been very well. Joan Helwys may even have been pregnant. There were perhaps several very practical reasons why travel may not have been advisable.
65. W.K.Jordan 'The Development of Religious Toleration in England' vol.2 footnote p.274
66. Jason Lee 'The Theology of John Smyth' p.49
67. J. Keith Cheetham 'On the trail of the Pilgrim Fathers' says (p.35) "Brewster made arrangements to charter a boat from Boston [in 1607]." Vernon Heaton 'The Mayflower' (p.38) prefers to see Brewster as the organiser of the Dutch ship in 1608
68. Sue Allan develops this very imaginatively in her recent historical novel 'Tudor Rose'.
69. Jason Lee 'The Theology of John Smyth' p.94. Lee uses the discussion with Helwys in Smyth's 'Last Book' to develop the idea that Smyth had been as generous as Helwys in assisting the poorer members of their congregation.
70. 'Of Religious Communion', chapter iii p.159 in volume 3 of 'The Works of John Robinson.'

CHAPTER 5

AMSTERDAM, LEIDEN, AND A BAPTIST CHURCH

When the Gainsborough and Scrooby Separatists eventually arrived in Amsterdam they found the Ancient Church of Francis Johnson already well established. Founded in 1597 the Church had recently laid out considerable sums of money in building an impressive new centre in which to worship[1].

Early writers[2] and even some more recent ones[3] believed that the new arrivals formally joined the Ancient Church. This seems unlikely given the nature of the covenants already established by the different congregations and the sheer number of people involved. Moreover, the Ancient Church already had an established leadership team and it would have been very difficult to graft onto that structure the new arrivals with their own burgeoning leadership. Most likely the new arrivals interacted with the Ancient Church but never joined.[4]

Whatever the precise nature of the relationship between the new and the old Separatists in Amsterdam, the fact remains that within a very short space of time they were falling out. No sooner had Smyth arrived in Amsterdam than he published (1608) his 'Differences of the churches of the Separation' in which he clearly laid out where he considered Johnson's Church was at fault. Never one to mince his words, Smyth informed Johnson (which could hardly have gone down well!) that Antichrist had not fully been exposed "and is exalted even in the true constituted churches."[5] Smyth went on to explain that his Church differed from "the ancient brethren of the Separation in the liturgy, presbytery and treasury of the church."[6]

The latter point is quite straightforward. Smyth objected to any suggestion that funds for the work of the Church could be collected from anyone other than the saints who constituted that Church. Outside funds, even from sympathetic or supportive individuals, broke the nature of the covenanted community. The issue over the presbytery was slightly more complicated. It wasn't simply that Smyth objected to the structure of leadership that had evolved in Johnson's Church, ("Pastors, teachers, rulers is none of God's ordinance but man's device")[7] it was that he objected to the shift in power represented by that arrangement. For Smyth, the power and authority in the Church should reside with the membership itself and not with the eldership. Famously, controversy focused on a verse in Matthew 18: 17. When Jesus told the disciples that in situations of dispute they should "tell it to the Church" Smyth understood this to mean the whole membership. Johnson, on the other hand, understood this to mean the eldership.[8]

But perhaps the most extraordinary element of disagreement between Smyth and the Ancient brethren was over the subject of worship. Here it is quite clear that Smyth had the novel views.

"We hold that the worship of the New Testament properly so called is spiritual, proceeding originally from the hart: and that reading out of a book (though a lawful ecclesiastical action) is no part of spiritual worship, but rather the invention of the man of synne."[9]

Obviously, one of the frequent objections of the Puritans in England had been the imposition of the Book of Common Prayer. The notion of reading out prayers was anathema to those who regarded praying as something that originated from within the heart. Amazingly, Smyth not only continued that reasoning and enforced it scrupulously, but he also applied the same principle to the Bible as well. And, while he considered it reasonable to refer to the Greek or Hebrew while expounding in public worship, he considered all translations to be works of man and therefore subject to the same restrictions as any other written aid to worship. They were to be avoided. Smyth considered it reasonable to make use of translations in personal devotions or in preparation for public 'spiritual' worship. But at the moment of spiritual worship all works of man must be removed and set aside.

It does seem extraordinary to us that Johnson, or anyone for that matter, could be accused of restricting the Spirit by using a Bible, but that was Smyth's position. And in an age when such differences really mattered, it was sufficient to impede any hope of mutual fellowship between the new and the old English Separatists in Amsterdam.

These were not the only issues that were causing strain between the two groups. The Ancient Church comprised men and women who originated mainly from London. The East Midlanders who comprised Smyth's congregation were, in the main, rural artisans and would have had little in common with Johnson's congregation.[10] Moreover, Johnson's congregation had been in Holland for a sufficient length of time for them to have adapted to the prevailing Dutch culture. Sunday observance was not as strict in Amsterdam as in England, and it began to appear that there were different social, cultural and moral outlooks that were dividing the old and the new Separatists.

There were also marked differences appearing between the Scrooby and Gainsborough Separatists themselves.

In February 1609 John Robinson made application to the Burgomasters of Leiden for permission to settle in their city with a number of his supporters. Permission was granted in April. While February was the date of the application, the research required to make this application, and the decision-making process that must have taken place before reaching such a momentous conclusion, suggests they must have been thinking about such a breach by the autumn of the previous year, which in Robinson's case could only be weeks after his arrival.

Stephen Wright believes there were differences between Smyth, Clyfton and Robinson before the emigration. These centred on differing emphases on the need for separation from the world and imposition of Church discipline.[11] But in addition to these disagreements there was a further issue that may well have been causing friction between the English Separatists, and that was over the matter of baptism.

W.T.Whitley saw the emergence of Separatist and then Baptist thinking as the logical outcome of discussion surrounding the nature of the Church.[12]

Once the Separatists had started to reject the validity of the Church of England it was but a short step to rejecting other aspects of that Church's ministry and sacraments. Smyth, in his debate with Richard Bernard ('Paralleles, Censures, Observations' 1609) was already moving in that direction. The Church of England was a 'false Church' according to Smyth, and its ministry and its worship were false. It was but a short step to conclude that its baptism was false as well.

Earlier Separatists had shown an ambivalence regarding the practice of infant baptism. The Barrowists refused to take their children to the Parish Church for baptism.[13] John Greenwood would not have his eighteen month old son, Adam, baptised until that baptism would be a true seal to a true covenant.[14] John Smyth had his two daughters, Chara and Sara, baptised at Gainsborough in 1604 and 1606 respectively,[15] but there is no evidence that Thomas Helwys had any of his children baptised after Thomas jnr. in 1603.[16] For those who had separated themselves from the Church of England because it was a false Church it was always going to be difficult to justify the baptism they had received through that false church. Smyth was to take that Separatist discomfort with baptism one step further.

He did this within weeks (if not days)[17] of the publication of 'Paralleles'. In a book entitled 'The Character of the Beast or the false constitution of the Church discovered' published in 1609, Smyth turned on Richard Clyfton as his sparring partner.

Smyth began by conceding that he had changed his mind rather a lot! But where truth is concerned, he wrote, then such things must happen. He came to the nub of the issue: "The false constitution is of infants baptized: we professe therefore that all those churches that baptize infants are of the same false constitution."[18] The churches of the Separation are no better than their mother England or their grandmother Rome. "No man can separate from England as a false Church except he do also separate from the baptism of England which giveth England her constitution."[19] In the batting backwards and forwards of scripture passages which Clyfton and Smyth embarked upon, Smyth maintained that since baptism was a baptism of repentance, and since infants could not possibly repent, then infants could not enter into a baptism of repentance.[20] Smyth's parting shot to his old friend and colleague was highly uncharitable: "I proclaim you are subtly blind and lead the blind after you into the ditch."[21]

That Smyth was writing so passionately in defence of believers' baptism in 1609 would strongly suggest that he had by this stage already renounced his earlier baptism by the Church of England. The most likely date for this new baptism was in or about January 1609.[22]

There have been attempts to date Smyth's baptism much earlier than this. In the nineteenth century a document emerged which purported to describe John Smyth's baptism at Epworth, England, in 1606. The document (sometimes referred to as the Crowle forgery) was good enough to fool John Clifford who published the details in the Baptist Magazine in 1879. Indeed historians right up to the mid nineteenth century were keen to date Smyth's baptism early.[23] In truth Smyth's conversion to Baptist thinking could only have happened AFTER he came to Amsterdam. The fellowship he maintained, albeit tentatively, with Johnson, Clyfton and Robinson on their arrival from England in 1608 was only possible while they shared a common understanding on baptism. The moment Smyth crossed the Rubicon and re-baptised himself then all semblance of union was ended. John Robinson may have decided it was time to part company with Smyth before the actual deed was done, but it would have been surprising if conversations about baptism had not already been taking place between them. Robinson knew Smyth well enough to know where such conversations were likely to lead. Richard Clyfton was to receive emissaries from the Smyth camp who tried to persuade him of the truth of believers' baptism.[24]

John Robinson provides the only contemporary account of Smyth's baptism. Writing in his work, 'On Religious Communion private and public' (1614) Robinson entitled chapter 4 'The outward baptism received in England is lawfully retained' and he provides this illuminating description:

"Mr Smyth, Mr Helwisse, and the rest, having utterly dissolved and disclaimed their former Church state and ministry, came together to erect a new Church by baptism; ..... and after some straining of courtesy who should begin …. Mr Smyth baptized first himself and next Mr Helwisse and so the rest making their particular confessions."[25]

The accusation that Smyth was a self or Se-Baptist was one that early Baptist historians were at great pains to discount. They clearly believed that such an action demeaned the practice of believers' baptism and discredited the witness of Smyth himself. Consequently Thomas Crosby, to be followed later by Ivimey, Taylor and Wood, proposed an alternative scenario:

"That first they formed a Church of their own opinion in the point of baptism; then the Church appoints two of their ministers to begin the administration of it, by baptising each other; after this one, or both these, baptize the rest of the congregation."[26]

Taylor went on to add the idea that they also practiced baptism by immersion[27]. This is certainly an anachronism. Baptism by immersion does not appear to have been practised until the 1630s or 1640s.[28] Smyth and Helwys' baptism would have been from a basin and by effusion.[29]

There was a further change that was taking place in the Smyth - Helwys group. When they left England they were both convinced Separatists and convinced Calvinists.[30] Having abandoned the Separatist concept of Church for the Baptist one they now began to move away from the major tenets of Calvinism.

During 1610[31] Smyth, along with Helwys, Murton and the rest of the Baptist Church, began to move towards a position that has often been described as Arminian.[32] In 'Corde Credimus' (April 1610) – Smyth's twenty article statement of faith[33] – the writer gives expression to his new range of ideas. Article 2 maintained that God had ordained all men to life and that no-one was reprobated. In Article 3 Smyth insisted that there was no such thing as Original Sin and that infants were born innocent. In Article 5 Smyth declared that the Grace of God was offered to all.

Smyth continued to give expression to these Arminian views in the rest of his published works. The most fulsome treatment was reserved for his English 'Confession of Faith' which ran to 100 articles and which was published after his death under the title 'Propositions and Conclusions.'[34] In this work Smyth opposed any notion of limited atonement (articles 28 & 35). And in at least ten articles he made statements that contradicted predestination or Original Sin. So, for example, in Article 18 we are told: "That original sin is an idle term, and that there is no such thing as men intend by the word." His reference to Ezekiel 18:20 indicated his belief in personal responsibility and his denial that any one person's sin could be transferred to another. Article 19 moreover insists that the death of Christ (a lamb slain from the beginning of the world) stopped the issue and passage of any sin that might have originated in Adam.

In 'Argumenta contra baptismum infantum' Smyth insisted, with some perception, that "It cannot be that Christ's redemption was more limited in scope than Adam's transgression."[35] And in writing in defence of the Mennonite leader Hans de Ries, Smyth wrote:

"If Christ redeems only certain men, He does not bruise the head of the serpent but the tail .... And therefore Christ's grace is inferior to Adam's sin because the latter ruined all men [but] the former delivered no more than a very few from destruction."[36]

Smyth's growing confidence in these ideas was matched by Thomas Helwys. Whatever disagreements they were about to enter into, they did at least share strong convictions in rejecting the principal tenets of Calvinism. Helwys was convinced that Christ died for all men and not merely for the elect. In 1611 he published a work with the transparent title, "A short and plain proof by the Word and works of God, that God's decree is not the cause of man's sin or condemnation, and that all men are redeemed by Christ as also that no infants are condemned." Helwys objected to predestination because "this causeth a slothful, careless, negligent profession" on the part of some and can cause others to "despair utterly" that there is no grace for them.[37] And in his most famous work, 'The Mystery of Iniquity', Helwys was to provide a most novel understanding of the concept of election.[38]

The origin of these Arminian views is hotly contested. It has been suggested that Smyth may have remembered them from his time in Cambridge when Peter Baro was popularising such views.[39] Whitley speculated that Smyth may have obtained the ideas from Robert Cooche.[40] While Stephen Brachlow muted the possibility that there was an in-built logic in the Puritan concept of the 'conditional covenant' which eventually worked through into a theology based on general atonement.[41] Undoubtedly there was a fierce debate ranging throughout Holland with the followers of Arminius and it would have been impossible for Smyth and Helwys not to have been brought into that debate.[42] For all that, however, the most likely source of these new Arminian ideas was the Dutch Mennonites in general and perhaps Hans de Ries in particular.[43] For while it is likely that Smyth and Helwys developed their ideas on baptism independently of the Mennonites it is stretching credulity to believe that the Arminian Mennonites did not have some responsibility for shifting Smyth and Helwys from their Calvinistic system. Helwys himself effectively admitted as much in one of his writings at this time.[44]

Mennonite influence was considerable on Smyth and Helwys. It was also to prove the cause of the irrevocable schism between the two English Baptists.

Postscript on the Ancient Church

Despite noble beginnings, the Ancient Church was to succumb to a series of sexual scandals[45] and devastating in-fighting. George Johnson became highly critical of his brother, Francis, and in particular of Francis' wife, Thomasine. He accused her of using "scent and starched linen" and being too much of the world.[46] George was eventually excommunicated. A more serious dispute then arose between Francis Johnson and Henry Ainsworth.[47] This was more doctrinal. Ainsworth was increasingly uncomfortable with the Presbyterian leanings of Johnson and the authority that was being invested in the eldership rather than the congregation. Ainsworth left the Church in 1610 and took a large group with him. He was replaced as teacher by Richard Clyfton who had refused to go with Robinson to Leiden on account of his age. In 1613 Ainsworth filed a lawsuit for possession of the Ancient Church's buildings and won the case. Johnson's group, now much depleted in numbers, was ordered to hand over the premises. They moved to Emden in Germany, although Clyfton didn't feel able to make the journey. He died in Amsterdam on 20th May 1616 and was buried in the old South Church.[48] William Bradford fondly remembered Clyfton as "a grave and fatherly old man when he came first into Holland having a great white beard .... [he] converted many to God by his faithful and painful ministry both in preaching and catechising, sound and orthodox he always was, and so continued to his end."[49]

When Francis Johnson died in Germany in 1617 the remnant that was left behind decided to emigrate to the New World. They boarded a ship in Gravesend bound for Virginia. Packed like herrings, by the time they arrived, in March 1619, approximately 130 out of 180 who set off had died.[50] Henry Ainsworth continued to lead the Ancient Church until his death in 1622.

Postscript on the Robinson Church at Leiden

About one hundred people settled in Leiden in 1609. This included a core of those like Brewster and Bradford who had come with Robinson from Scrooby, and also a number who had come from the Ancient Church disillusioned by the moral failures and constant bickering. By 1620 this number had grown to over four hundred people, made up largely of new arrivals from England. Between a quarter and a third of them appear to have come from the Norwich region and may well have had contact with Robinson when he served there.[51]

In 1611 a large house was purchased, known as the Green Door.[52] It was in Bell Alley and acted both as a meeting place for the Separatists and also as accommodation for Robinson and his family. The property had a significant amount of land on which smaller dwelling places were constructed for the benefit of members of the congregation.

Leiden worked well for Robinson. Its University recognised his talents and made use of him, for example, in the debates with the

Remonstrants.[53] Robinson was made an honorary member of the University in 1615.[54] Leiden also worked well for William Brewster. He became an English tutor[55] as well as Managing Director of the Pilgrim Press which produced a plethora of works released into England promoting the Puritan and Separatist cause.[56]

William Bradford, however, explained how the problems associated with life in Leiden began to outweigh the advantages.[57] The Separatists were engaged in hard manual labour to make ends meet. There were real concerns about the moral welfare of the young who were adopting the prevailing values of contemporary Dutch society. The openings for the Gospel were increasingly restricted. And the whole dream of a Christian society, which had brought many of them from England in the first place, were only to be realised in a new environment in which they could control their own destiny. It is also possible that the timing of their eventual decision to leave was influenced by a bout of persecution they were receiving as foreigners in the city.[58]

Negotiations to emigrate had started in 1617.[59] But planning arrangements, securing passage, and last minute hitches meant that it was not until July 1620 that 55 out of the 300 Leiden congregation left Holland for England on the Speedwell. And it was not until the September that a total of 102 passengers left Plymouth aboard the Mayflower.[60] Their passage to New England took 65 days. The Pilgrim Fathers,[61] as they eventually became known, endured that first winter but at a terrible cost. By November 1621 they had seen 51 of their number die.

John Robinson never made the journey to America. He died in Leiden on 1st March 1625. (Both King James I and William Hickman also died that same year.)[62] William and Mary Brewster brought two of their children, Love and Wrestling, with them to America in 1620. Their three other children, Jonathan, Patience, and Fear came over in 1621 and 1623.[63] William Brewster died on 18th April 1643 aged nearly 80. He had travelled a long way from his Manor House in Scrooby. William Bradford affectionately remembered his aged mentor. He had "borne his part in weal and woe with this poor persecuted church above 36 years in England, Holland and in this wilderness, and done the Lord and them faithful service in his place and calling."[64] William Bradford himself, born in Austerfield in 1590 and an early member of John Smyth's covenanted Gainsborough – Scrooby Church, was appointed the second governor of the newly established Plymouth Plantation. He served in that capacity for 33 years in total, and died in 1656.[65]

Footnotes

1. Edmund Jessup 'The Mayflower Story' p.11
2. Thomas Crosby 'The History of the English Baptists' vol.1 p.91 not only says that Smyth joined Ainsworth's Church but that the Church subsequently excommunicated him when he began "to entertain some principles different from his brethren." W.K.Jordan 'Development of Religious Toleration in England' vol.2 writing in 1936 says that Smyth and his followers emigrated to Holland "where they joined Johnson's company of Separatists." p.263
3. Vernon Heaton 'The Mayflower' p.41; E. Catherine Anwyl 'John Smyth.' Whitley 'Works' p.lxxxii says that the new arrivals kept apart from the Ancient Church but "naturally lived on sisterly terms." David Beale 'The Mayflower Pilgrims' p.64 says that Smyth and his group "worshipped with the Ancient Church" but doesn't suggest the two groups joined together.
4. Burgess 'Smyth, Helwys and the first Baptist Church in England' p.98; Jason Lee 'The Theology of John Smyth' p.53
5. Found in Whitley 'The Works of John Smyth' p.270
6. Whitley 'Works' p.271
7. Whitley 'Works' p.271
8. Whitley 'Works' p.425-437
9. Whitley 'Works' p.271
10. Burgess 'Smyth, Helwys' p.98
11. Stephen Wright 'Early English Baptists' p.22. John Smyth adopted a zero tolerance approach: "No religious communion to be had but with members of a visible church."('Principles and Inferences') Robinson was not inclined to be so harsh.
12. Whitley 'A History of British Baptists' p.18: "For the sources of Baptist life we need to look to the Scriptures in the vernacular, and to the consequent emergence of questions about the Church."
13. Barrie White EST p.79
14. Barrie White EST p.80
15. David Beale 'Mayflower Pilgrims' p.46 footnote 10
16. In an article for the Nottinghamshire Guardian on Broxtowe Hall available at www.nottshistory.org.uk/articles/villagepacks/broxtowehall.htm
17. Barrie White EST p.131 who quotes Henry Ainsworth's opinion.
18. Whitley 'Works' p.565

19. Whitley 'Works' p.566
20. Whitley 'Works' p.567
21. Whitley 'Works' p.680
22. Jason Lee 'The Theology of John Smyth' p.77-78. Champlin Burrage 'Early English Dissenters' p.240 dates Smyth's baptism to December 1608 or January 1609. Coggins 'John Smyth's Congregation' p.63-65 sets February 1609 (the time of Robinson's departure) as the latest possible date, but concedes the baptism could have taken place as early as the close of 1608.
23. J.H.Wood 'History of the Baptists' following Adam Taylor's 'History of the General Baptists' dates the flight to Holland in 1606 and the formation of Smyth's Baptist Church as 1607.
24. Burgess 'Smyth, Helwys' p.149 contains a letter from Clyfton in which he describes the approach of Edward Southworth and Hugh Bromhead to tackle him about his views on baptism.
25. In the 'Works of John Robinson' vol.3 p.168
26. Thomas Crosby 'The History of the English Baptists' p.99
27. Adam Taylor 'The History of the General Baptists' vol.1 p.70
28. While this is standard Baptist history, Champlin Burrage EED p.277-278 noted that Leonard Busher, in 'Religion's Peace' , (1615), did seem to advocate baptism by immersion: such as willingly and gladly receive the word of salvation, Christ "hath commanded to be baptized in the water, that is, dipped for dead in the water." Stephen Wright (BQ 39 p.181) agrees that Busher may well have been engaged in this practice even before the Mennonites.
29. Barrie White EST p.133 quoting Bishop Joseph Hall. Dexter and Dexter 'The England and Holland of the Pilgrims' (1905) were not sympathetic to the Baptists. They include a description of the baptism p.455-456 which may or may not approximate to what happened:

    "They met where they were accustomed to worship, included in the furniture of which room was a three legged stool which held a basin of water. Ranging themselves around this stool and without a preliminary prayer Smyth dipped up water in his hand and poured it over his own forehead in the name of the Father, Son and Holy Ghost. Then he repeated the ceremony in the case of each of the others."

    According to Dexter and Dexter they ended by a celebration of the Lord's Supper "and at last they felt themselves a genuine Church of Christ, if the only one upon earth." p.457
30. Barrie White 'The English Baptists of the 17th Century' p.23
31. Burgess 'Smyth, Helwys' p.176 says that it was "in the closing months of 1609" that Smyth and his Church began to give "careful consideration to some of the points in controversy between the Calvinists and Arminians."
32. Nicholas Tyacke 'Anti-Calvinists' 1987 p.245 points out that the term 'Arminian' "does not mean that the Dutch Theologian Jacobus Arminius was normally the source of the ideas so labelled. Rather 'Arminian' denotes a

coherent body of anti-Calvinist religious thought which was gaining ground in various regions of early seventeenth century Europe. Arminianism itself can plausibly be understood as part of a more widespread philosophical scepticism engendered by way of reaction to the dogmatic certainties of the sixteenth century reformation." In truth, Arminianism was only a modified version of Calvinism. Arminians would have accepted most tenets of Protestantism but insisted upon general not limited atonement, and would have questioned the irresistible nature of God's grace and the inevitable perseverance of the saints. Today most Christians would probably be Arminian in outlook but would barely understand the nuances. In the seventeenth century Christians could kill one another over such differences.

33. This Short Confession of Faith can be accessed on the internet at www.rpc.ox.ac.uk/ohp/jsmyth.htm

34. Smyth's one hundred 'Propositions and Conclusions' are printed in Burgess 'Smyth, Helwys' p.241-257

35. Found in Jason Lee 'Theology of John Smyth' p.176

36. Found in Jason Lee 'Theology of John Smyth' p.178

37. From Burgess 'Smyth, Helwys' p.222-223

38. 'A Short declaration of the Mystery of Iniquity' ed. Richard Groves p.66-67: Helwys uses 'election' not in the classic Calvinistic sense of God's predetermined choosing but rather in the more modern sense of electing or choosing someone: "How blessed and comfortable a thing were it for a holy people so to elect their pastor that should lead them …. And what a blessed comfort were it for a holy man to be so elected of a holy people."

39. Barrie White 'The English Baptists of the 17th Century' p.24

40. Whitley in 'History of the British Baptists' p.28 notes the similarity of views on free will between Smyth and Robert Cooche who had written against Calvin in 1551. But he concedes it unlikely that Smyth had ever read any of Robert Cooche's works. However, by the time Whitley came to write his article in the BQ vol.vii 1934-35 'Thomas Helwys of Grays Inn' he maintains that some of Helwys' theological views show clear signs of influence if not direct borrowing from Robert Cooke, "an Anabaptist and courtier of Edward VI who had taken a strong stand against the antinomian implications of Calvin's teachings."

41. In Jason Lee 'The Theology of John Smyth' p.182

42. Barrie White 'The English Baptists of the 17th Century' p.24

43. Jason Lee 'The Theology of John Smyth' p.194. Coggins 'John Smyth's Congregation' p.72-73 reminds us that de Ries was in charge of the Alkmaar congregation some 20 miles from Amsterdam, but as an elder in the Waterlander Mennonites he would have had some authority over, and contact with, the Amsterdam congregation. Hans de Ries' wife was English so he would have probably acquired sufficient English to communicate with John Smyth.

44. In 'An Advertisement or admonition unto the congregations' (Amsterdam 1611) Helwys thanked the Waterlander Mennonites for "discovering our errors." Stephen Wright EEB p.38 concludes that Helwys could only be

referring to their Arminian insights since Helwys publicly rejected most other Mennonite ideas.

45. Edmund Jessup 'The Mayflower Story' p.11 provides fascinating details.
46. David Beale 'The Mayflower Pilgrims' p.65
47. David Beale 'The Mayflower Pilgrims' p.65-66
48. Edmund Jessup 'The Mayflower Story' p.12
49. Quote found in David Beale 'Mayflower Pilgrims' p.68
50. Barrie White EST p.155
51. Coggins 'John Smyth's Congregation' p.66
52. David Beale 'The Mayflower Pilgrims' p.70-71
53. The Remonstrants were adherents of Jacob Arminius' modified Calvinism. Their charter of beliefs (The Remonstrance) was roundly condemned at the Synod of Dort and they were harshly treated.
54. Edmund Jessup 'The Mayflower Story' p.13
55. J. Keith Cheetham 'On the trail of the Pilgrim Fathers' p.43
56. Edmund Jessup 'The Mayflower Story' p.13
57. William Bradford 'Of Plymouth Plantation' chapter 4
58. David Beale in 'The Mayflower Pilgrims' p.74 covers this unpleasantness, and quotes from Professor Jan Van Dorsten of the University of Leiden who notes that "the violence of this incident towards non-conformists in general must have strengthened the resolve of the Pilgrims to leave."
59. David Beale 'The Mayflower Pilgrims' p.79
60. Edmund Jessup 'The Mayflower Story' p.17
61. Edmund Jessup 'The Mayflower Story' p.15-16 tells us that "For many years subsequent generations in New England referred to their heroic ancestors as First Comers or Fore-fathers." It wasn't until 1793 when Rev Chandler Robbins referred to them as 'Pilgrims' picking up an expression from Hebrews 11:13. William Bradford ('Of Plymouth Plantation') had drawn upon this verse of scripture, "So they left the goodly and pleasant city which had been their resting place near twelve years: but they knew they were pilgrims."
62. David Beale 'The Mayflower Pilgrims' p.82. The 'Mayflower Trail' information board outside the Parish Church at Sturton le Steeple says that Robinson died of the plague.
63. David Beale 'The Mayflower Pilgrims' p.114
64. William Bradford 'Of Plymouth Plantation' p.359
65. Francis Murphy in his introduction to Bradford's 'Of Plymouth Plantation' p.xiii

CHAPTER 6

THE PARTING OF THE WAYS AND
THE MYSTERY OF INIQUITY

Once again John Smyth changed his mind. Having taking the momentous step to un-church himself and take a new baptism, Smyth came to regret his actions within a matter of weeks.[1] The argument employed to justify the new baptism was based on the absence of any true Church according to the pattern Smyth and his friends had mapped out. To say that they were unaware of the existence of the Mennonites at this time is nonsense.[2] The bake-house they had been living in belonged to Jan Munter, one of the Mennonite community.[3] And Hans de Ries would have been well known to Smyth and Helwys. The decision not to seek baptism from the Mennonites stemmed not from ignorance of their existence but doubts as to their orthodoxy. During 1609, as his contact with and knowledge of the Mennonites increased, Smyth became convinced that he had been in error over the decision to baptise himself and create a new Church. Rather, he considered it would be more appropriate for his congregation of perhaps 50 people to join the Mennonites and put right their earlier mistake.

In February 1610 John Smyth sought union with the Mennonites. He and a number of others presented a petition to the Waterlander Mennonites asking that they be admitted to membership "and be brought back to the true Church of Christ as quickly as may be suffered."[4]

Thomas Helwys profoundly disagreed. He and ten others seceded from Smyth's congregation.[5] The gist of Helwys' objections can be found in one of three works he was to produce in 1611. 'An advertisement or admonition unto the congregations which men call the New Fryelers'[6] blamed the Mennonites for corrupting Smyth and leading him astray. Helwys identified four main errors.

Firstly, he was not at all convinced about the Mennonite Christology with its suggestion that Christ did not obtain his flesh from Mary. Secondly he believed that the Sabbath should be a day of rest and should be kept holy every first day of the week, something he did not believe the Mennonites took sufficiently seriously. Thirdly, he was scathing about the Mennonites' opposition to Christians serving as magistrates. For Helwys, the magistrate was fulfilling a godly duty and he had no truck with those who preferred to retreat from society and abandon social responsibility. Fourthly, and more pressing than any of the above issues, was the matter of Successionism.

Helwys was mindful of Jesus' words (Matthew 18:20) that "where two or three are gathered together in my name there am I in the midst." This demonstrated to Helwys' satisfaction that independent churches of two or three people were ecclesial entities in their own right. For John Smyth to feel the need to join a pre-existent Church implied some deficiency in the way they had been constituted, and hinted at some return to the older understanding of Church they had suffered to come out from. Helwys was incensed. In a letter to the Mennonites in spring 1610 he referred to Successionism as "Antichrist's chief hold."[7] Quite recently Stephen Copson succinctly and astutely summarised the difference between Smyth and Helwys over this crucial matter: "For Smyth, the church preceded baptism; for Helwys, baptism formed the church."[8]

There may have been other reasons behind Helwys' separation from Smyth. Stephen Wright maintains that politics, not theology, lay at the heart of their dispute.[9] Helwys, as a member of the English gentry and ruling class, felt social order was being threatened by the undermining not only of the magistracy but the Sabbath as well. James Coggins sees a further factor contributing to the disagreement. "The Smyth congregation" he maintains, "was not the only congregation in history to experience a power struggle between a spiritual leader and a wealthy member paying the bills."[10]

But genuine theological differences were at stake in this clash, and not just over the nature of the Church. For while Helwys had been in agreement with Smyth in their move away from Calvinism towards a position of general atonement, he began to detect in some of Smyth's writings a move further than this. In particular Helwys accused Smyth of exalting free will to a degree he did not feel warranted.

John Smyth's 'Propositions and Conclusions' – a one hundred article statement of faith – was to contain several explosive and controversial passages. At considerable length Smyth denies the existence of original sin and advocates a degree of human self determination. Article 14 insisted that "God created man with freedom of will so that he had the ability to choose the good and eschew the evil …. and that this freedom of will was a natural faculty or power created by God in the soul of man." He went on to say in article 17 that "Adam being fallen did not lose any natural power or faculty which God created in his soul … being fallen he still retained freedom of will."[11]

These articles were not published until after Smyth's death but provide an indication of his teaching at the time. Helwys was decidedly uncomfortable with the direction Smyth was travelling. A second of Helwys' works of 1611, "A Short and Plain Proof," was a reaffirmation of his belief in general atonement: that Christ died for all men. But at the end of the work Helwys refers to "that gross and fearful error of free will" and rejects any suggestion "that man hath any free will or power in himself to work his own salvation or choose life."[12]

The Waterlander Mennonites were in a dilemma over the application from Smyth's congregation. Hans de Ries had drawn up a 'Short Confession' of 38 articles outlining their basic teachings. To show their genuine desire to unite with the Mennonites, Smyth and his congregation signed this Confession of Faith. Smyth followed this by the publication of his own Latin confession of faith in 20 articles, 'Corde Credimus', for the consideration of the Mennonites, and to demonstrate the degree of common ground between them.

The Amsterdam Mennonites, however, were not free agents. As part of a wider Association (the Broederschap) they needed outside permission to receive the Smyth congregation into their membership without a further baptism. Such permission was hard to obtain,[13] and union was only to happen once the Broederschap had broken down.[14]

In response to all this Thomas Helwys published his own Declaration of Faith in 1611.[15] It maps out clear areas of difference between his own Baptist understanding and that of Smyth and the Mennonites. The longest section deals with the positive role of the magistracy, "a Holy ordinance of God" which is in marked contrast to Smyth's 'Propositions and Conclusions.' The latter has only two out of one hundred articles on the role of the magistrate, one which tells the magistrate not to meddle in religion and the other which describes the magistracy as a "permissive ordinance of God."[16]

Helwys also affirms the ecclesial validity of small congregations, "though they be but two or three" with the clear implication that it is unnecessary to belong to a larger and established congregation.

The main sections of Helwys' Confession, however, show again clear signs of rowing backwards from Smyth on the central theological issues. Helwys avoids any mention of free will, and seems to return to the old idea of original sin: through Adam's sin, all men sinned "his sin being imputed to all." "Men are by nature children of wrath, born in iniquity and in sin conceived."

Thomas Helwys was attempting to put some clear distance between his own theological ideas and those of his former pastor.

Smyth meanwhile was seriously ill. He would appear to have been suffering from tuberculosis, a condition not helped by the dampness of the Norfolk fens or the waterways of Holland.[17] As a physician he would have been well aware of the symptoms and the inevitable outcome.

In 1612 work began on 'The Last Book of John Smith: called the retraction of his errors and the confirmation of the truth.'[18] It was a book he never finished and was left to his friends to conclude and publish.[19] 'The Last Book' is unlike anything Smyth had produced before. In it he adopts a wholly different, more sanguine and conciliatory tone. He regrets that "in the days of my blind zeal .... I was somewhat lavish in censuring and judging others." He apologises for the use of intemperate language. And while he still cannot accept the Church of England as a true, visible Church, he concedes that there are men of good conscience within its structures and he will no longer refer to them as Antichristian. He regrets "all those biting and bitter words" "as not being of the Spirit of Christ." And he especially apologises to Richard Bernard for the harsh tone he adopted in 'Paralleles'. Regarding those of the Separation he says: "I should have with the Spirit of meekness instructed them … but my words have been stout and mingled with gall."

Smyth did take exception in the 'Last Book' to being accused by Thomas Helwys of blaspheming against the Holy Ghost.[20] But the tone that prevails is one of high minded quietism:

"And now from this day forward do I put an end to all controversies and questions about the outward church and ceremonies with all men."

Smyth, throughout this book, reflects an irenic tone that demonstrates the profound influence of the Mennonites on his style as well as his thinking. Peacefulness was not something he had witnessed in the fractious relations of the English Separatists. But it was something he learned from increased exposure to the teachings and example of the Waterlander Mennonites.[21]

John Smyth died in August 1612. He was buried on 1st September at the Niewe Kerke in Amsterdam.[22] In 1615 his congregation were finally received into membership of the Waterlander Mennonites,[23] eventually merging with these Dutch Christians and disappearing as an entity in their own right.[24]

Before he died Smyth would probably have seen a copy of a book Thomas Helwys had prepared for publication.[25] It was entitled, 'A Short Declaration of the Mystery of Iniquity.' The book was written and printed in Holland but was intended for an English audience.

The 'Mystery of Iniquity' was a phrase found in 2 Thessalonians 2:7. Helwys took it to mean unrighteousness masquerading as righteousness. John Smyth had used the image in his writings. The work is effectively an attack on every known religious viewpoint

Helwys could think of. Walter Burgess was to accurately summarise the content of the book when he wrote:

"The Roman Catholic Church was wrong, the Anglican Church was wrong, Puritanism was wrong, Brownism was wrong, John Robinson in particular was wrong. Helwys had caught a vision of the truth, and the stupendous task of setting the world right had been laid upon him."[26]

The tone of the book is savage, its contents mediocre. It is repetitive and tedious, with little literary merit. Whitley fairly assesses the book as "incoherent."[27] And yet there are perhaps two themes which were to take on enormous significance.

One of these is the theme of religious liberty. John Smyth had briefly touched on this theme in his one hundred articles of faith (Article 84), although he never developed the idea.[28] Hitherto most religious groups, including Robinson and the Separatists, were keen to advocate religious freedom provided it was only for their particular version of the truth![29] Indeed most were willing to advocate the use of force to impose their version of the truth. But now Helwys was to make a statement that was both profound and far reaching. In Book Two of 'Mystery' Helwys argues that the authority of the King is restricted simply to secular matters. The King has no right to intervene in spiritual matters and no right "to force men's conscience in their religion to God." "Men should choose their religion themselves." If the King were to compel people to worship against their conscience then he would be compelling them to sin against God.[30]

"For our Lord the king is but an earthly king, and he has no authority as a king but in earthly causes .... Men's religion to God is between God and themselves, the king shall not answer for it. Neither may the king be judge between God and man. Let them be heretics, Turks, Jews, or whatsoever, it appertains not to the earthly power to punish them in the least measure."[31]

This perceptive and insightful statement has justly become famous. It laid the groundwork for much more fulsome expositions of the rights of conscience and religious liberty. It was pioneering in extending freedom of worship even to those outside of the Christian faith. Later Baptist writers such as Leonard Busher and Roger Williams were more eloquent in their treatment of the subject. But Helwys deserves the credit for producing the first published defence of religious liberty in English.[32] There is a striking irony that a statement which has earned Helwys the reputation as the champion of religious toleration and freedom should emerge from a book which is dripping poison on every page and is grossly intolerant.

The origins of these views on religious freedom have been variously argued over. Some have seen them as a product of Smyth and Helwys sampling the air of Dutch freedom after the crippling effects of binding men's consciences in England.[33] Others, unsurprisingly, have seen further evidence of Mennonite influence on the course of English Baptist history.[34] Or it could simply be that this "highly developed sense of the sovereignty of the individual conscience"[35] was a natural and logical corollary of the personalisation of religion that had been the mark of the Baptists' spiritual quest.

There was, however, a second hugely important theme located in 'Mystery of Iniquity'. This emerges most clearly in the Appendix when Helwys goes on the attack against the Separatists in Amsterdam and Leiden. He insists that the Biblical injunction to flee persecution was not to escape harm but in order better to proclaim the Gospel.[36] He has become convinced that in escaping England they had abandoned their responsibility of witnessing for the truth. They had become cowards sheltering in the place of safety whereas they should be back in Satan's strongholds promoting the truth as they understood it.[37]

Helwys' conviction on this point was one that he took extremely seriously. And even as he wrote those words he and the ten others with him were preparing to return back to England to witness for the truth. In a rather poignant passage Helwys declares:

"Let none think we are altogether ignorant what building, what warfare we take in hand, and that we have not sat down and in some measure thoroughly considered what the cost and the danger may be. Also let none think that we are without sense and feeling of our inability to begin and our weakness to endure to the end the weight and danger of such a work."[38]

John Robinson took exception to Helwys' accusations. In his 'Of Religious Communion' he dedicates chapter three to the subject 'Of flight and persecution.' Robinson provides the examples of Jacob, Moses and David in the Old Testament to prove the necessity of flight under certain circumstances.[39] He then rounded on Helwys with a withering attack. Helwys isn't returning to England for religious reasons:

"But more than likely it is that, having scattered the people by his heady and indiscreet courses and otherwise disabled himself, that natural confidence which abounded in him, took occasion, under an appearance of spiritual courage, to press him upon those desperate courses which he, of late, hath run."[40]

Robinson was of the opinion that Helwys had made such a mess of things in Holland, and had alienated virtually everyone, that he could not stay any longer. The only course left for him was return.[41]

This is probably a little uncharitable. James Coggins, however, is certainly of the mind that Helwys did not really fit in Holland. He didn't speak the language and, unlike Smyth, did not want to become part of Dutch society. Helwys' refusal to join the Mennonites was in part a matter of wanting to stay English. "One suspects that what really decided the matter for Helwys were his natural prejudices and inclinations."[42] In all of this there might have been one overriding personal reason for Helwys to return home: the hope of once again seeing his wife and family.[43]

There were other factors that might have had a bearing on the timing of their return. Archbishop Bancroft died in November 1610. His successor, George Abbot, was known to be more sympathetic to the Puritan views and was to tolerate far more religious freedom within the Church of England than his predecessor.[44] Moreover, the public burning of the Baptist Edward Wightman (April 11th 1612) so appalled right minded people that almost immediately legislation was put in place to prevent such an occurrence from happening again.[45]

Helwys' chosen destination was London. He had no home in Nottingham after the King had sequestrated Broxtowe Hall.[46] He did, however, have family in London: a cousin Gervase and an uncle Geoffrey both of whom were men of position in Court circles.[47] And Helwys did indeed appear to be deadly earnest about his quest to take the truth right to the centre of power.

Helwys wrote 'The Mystery of Iniquity' in Holland. He brought the manuscript over to England where he had it published.[48] The precise number of people who came with him to England is uncertain. James Coggins was only positively able to identify John and Jane Murton, Thomas Seamer and William Pygott.[49] At some point in 1612 two things happened. Firstly, Helwys re-formed his Church in Spitalfields, just outside the city walls of London, thus forming the first known Baptist Church on English soil. Secondly, Helwys tried to present a copy of his latest work to King James. According to Jason Lee,[50] when this attempt failed he added a handwritten note in the flyleaf of one of the copies asking for the King's attention to his work. It is this copy that has been preserved in the Bodleian Library in Oxford. It included the following memorable words:

"The king is a mortal man and not God, therefore hath no power over the immortal souls of his subjects to make laws and ordinances for them, and to set spiritual lords over them."

Helwys signed his note, "Tho. Helwys. Spitalfield near London." Richard Groves writes: "It is not known whether King James received the book or, if he received it, read it. It is widely assumed, however, that the book and the note sealed Thomas Helwys' fate."[51]

Another account is found in a recent internet site:

"Helwys presented a copy of 'Mystery' to King James I who took little pleasure in the questionable theological opinions expressed. The work was promptly ordered to be seized and burned …. Helwys was arrested and questioned …. Unwilling to recant Helwys was thrown into prison in 1613."[52]

From this point everything is unclear. According to tradition, Thomas Helwys was sent to Newgate prison either for his effrontery in trying to deal with the King or for the ideas contained within his book. But I can find no corroborating evidence to prove Helwys was in <u>Newgate</u> prison. The first suggestion of his fate appeared in Whitley's 'History of the British Baptists' in 1923. Neither Burgess or Burrage or indeed Whitley's earlier works make reference to <u>Newgate</u> prison. And Whitley's assumption seems only to be based on the slightly better attested fact that John Murton was in Newgate prison by 1613.[53] W.K.Jordan, interestingly, agreed that Murton was imprisoned in 1613 but states that Helwys was probably not taken into custody until the following year.[54] But he again does not specify which prison.

Walter Burgess was convinced that Thomas Helwys was still alive in 1614. This was because John Robinson replied to Helwys' accusations in 'Mystery of Iniquity' in his work of 1614 'Of Religious Communion', and it was clear from the tone of the work that Robinson assumed Helwys was very much alive. Interestingly, Robert Ashton, who edited the 1851 edition of Robinson's works and who provides some introductory notes about Helwys, says:

"Nothing is known of his history after the year 1612 beyond the fact of his labouring zealously in His master's cause and his suffering greatly for righteousness' sake till 1620 when he was released from his labours and trials by the hand of death."[55]

Adam Taylor believed that Helwys was still writing Baptist treatises in 1618 and claimed to be able to trace correspondence of his as late as 1622.[56] But since Taylor seemed to have got most things about Helwys wrong we can assume this is inaccurate also!

Stephen Wright is prepared to identify Helwys as the author of 'Objections: answered by way of dialogue' which appeared in 1615.[57] If Helwys did write this (and not Murton) then Wright concedes Helwys was probably ill at the time and was certainly dead by the end of the year.

The most measured dating of the death of Thomas Helwys was provided by Walter Burgess. In his article in the Transactions of the Baptist Historical Society 1912/13 Burgess notes that the will of Geoffrey Helwys (Thomas' uncle) was dated April 8th 1616. In it he makes the following bequest: "I give to Johane Elwes widdowe lat wife of Thomas Elwes deceased tenne pounds." Burgess concludes "The death of Thomas Helwys was recent, and we shall not be far wrong in assigning it to the year 1615."[58]

As an interesting aside, Champlin Burrage also makes reference to a small piece of paper he found in the Library of the House of Lords. He dates it about 1614. The paper is entitled 'A Most Humble Supplication of divers poore prisoners and many others the kinges majesty's loyal subjects…"[59] The Supplication is neatly written and addressed "To the right honourable assembly of the commons – House of Parliament" and it is signed "By his majestys faithful subjects most falsely called Anabaptists."

The petition states that the suppliants are willing to take the Oath of Allegiance but the bishops will not let them. Bitterly they complain:

"Kept have we been by them many years in lingering imprisonments, divided from wives, children, servants and callings, not for any other cause but only for conscience towards God, to the utter undoing of wives and children."

The petition was rejected. Burrage maintains, "The handwriting may be that of Thomas Helwys."[60]

John Murton has been described as Helwys' "chief helper."[61] I have been intrigued by the fact that Murton is described as the leader of this congregation of Baptists as early as 1613 while he was still in prison, and while Helwys presumably was still alive.[62]

A further speculation

Newgate was not the only prison that held religious dissidents. The Fleet prison, the Marshalsea, and the Clink all operated at this time and held notorious Protestant and Catholic dissenters. Incarceration in prison might seem the end to any active campaign but in fact earlier generations of dissenters had managed very successfully to carry on their writing and publishing from gaol, Barrow and Greenwood perhaps being the most famous examples.[63]

Visitors were allowed; gifts exchanged; and writing permitted. Some of the terms of imprisonment would have allowed considerable room for manoeuvre.[64] John Murton seems to have functioned as leader of the Spitalfields Baptist congregation while serving several spells of imprisonment.

Indeed the nature of Thomas Helwys' imprisonment is interesting. Unless his crimes were judged so heinous that he was never to be released, it would have been more usual for him to suffer a short prison sentence. An article on Broxtowe Hall in the Nottinghamshire Guardian (found in the EMBA Archive) says there are "several references" to his confinement in prison which might indicate (like Murton) not one long prison sentence but several shorter ones.

A second speculation

In spite of being referred to as a 'Baptist woman'[65] there is no evidence to prove that Joan Helwys ever agreed with her husband's position on believers' baptism or his move away from Calvinism. The shift from a Separatist to a Baptist mode of thinking was one that took place while Joan was absent, and it may have been one she did not feel able to make. James Coggins may have listed Joan as a member of Thomas' congregation in England[66] but I suspect that inclusion is more out of sentiment than evidence. It is possible that Joan's position may have been similar to that of Lady Isabel Bowes. Helwys dedicated his 'Short and Plain proofe' to Lady Isabel on 2nd June 1611. She was well known to Helwys and had helped orchestrate the critical meeting at her Coventry home in 1606. Helwys refers to "the faithful and loving respect I bear to you" and tells her that "I know there is none in the land that hath better means to procure a cause of religion to be handled according to the judgement of the best."[67] Despite the flattery Lady Isabel was not persuaded by any of Helwys' arguments. She not only remained in the Church of England but she also remained a Calvinist to the end.[68]

The romantic in us all might agree with Ernest Payne: "We can but hope that before or during his imprisonment Helwys again saw his wife and children."[69] But there is always the possibility that Joan Helwys felt grievously let down by her husband. The fact that she disappears from all records may well have been a deliberate attempt on her part to distance herself from her husband's views.

Of some interest is the fate of one of the other 'Baptist women,' Jane Murton, wife of Helwys' successor John Murton. Loyally she followed her husband from the Smyth camp to the Helwys camp, and from Amsterdam to London. But when her husband died in 1630 within a very short space of time she returned to Amsterdam and joined her old friends worshipping in the Bake-house.[70]

A third speculation

Thomas Pygott[71] is believed to have published John Smyth's 'Last Book' and to have led Smyth's congregation after his death. There were several other members of the Pygott family involved in Smyth's congregation. William Pygott, however, was part of the group that left Smyth and joined Helwys. Did the division between Smyth and Helwys divide a family? There are problems associated with the different spellings of the surname. There could have been contemporary variations. But Whitley (see my footnote 24 at the end of this chapter) has several different spellings. This raises interesting possibilities. On 11th April 1608 back in Nottinghamshire Helwys and his wife were cited in the Archdeaconry presentment books for non-attendance at their Parish Church. Other people were charged with them including Helwys' servant whose last name was 'Pigot'. This may, of course, be pure coincidence, and there may be no connection between this man and the Pygotts found with Smyth and Helwys in

Amsterdam. No Christian name is provided for the servant 'Pigot' in 1608, but there may be a very outside chance that this man was the same William Pygott, the old family retainer, who stayed with Helwys when others did not, and who loyally followed his master back to England.

Footnotes

1. Stephen Wright 'Early English Baptists' (EEB) p.35
2. Stephen Wright EEB p.34: "the idea that Smyth was unaware of their existence is risible."
3. While Coggins 'John Smyth's Congregation' has questioned the date when Smyth's congregation moved into the bake-house, he makes the point (p.72) that when they did move into the building it would not have been empty. It may have already had some "old and necessitous" Waterlander Mennonites living there. The bake-house was effectively a Mennonite poorhouse. Interaction and familiarisation with the Waterlanders would have happened at a very early stage.
4. Jason Lee 'The Theology of John Smyth' p.87
5. Technically speaking Helwys' ten excommunicated Smyth's thirty two (Whitley 'Works' p.108). J. Glenwood Clayton 'Thomas Helwys: a Baptist Founding Father' believes there might have been twelve with Helwys. Coggins 'John Smyth's Congregation' p.77-81 believes it was more complicated than that. He believes that the split between Smyth and Helwys may have happened BEFORE the application to join the Mennonites, and there were perhaps a dozen people who were uncertain which side to join. Smyth's 'thirty two' was based on the number of his followers who signed the application to join. There were forty three people who later signed the Waterlander Confession of Faith which suggests that all the waverers were won over by Smyth.
6. See Burgess 'Smyth, Helwys' p.226-227. Burgess says that the 'Advertisement or admonition' was intended for the New Fryesers or Frisian Anabaptists. 'Fryelers' is a mistaken reading. Whitley 'History of British Baptists' p.32 however, believes that Fryelers is a strange spelling of 'Free-willers'
7. Jason Lee 'The Theology of John Smyth' p.87
8. Baptist Quarterly (BQ) 41 no.6 April 2006 p.371
9. Stephen Wright EEB p.54
10. Coggins 'John Smyth's Congregation' p.111
11. Burgess 'Smyth, Helwys' p.239ff prints the 100 'Propositions and Conclusions'
12. Burgess 'Smyth, Helwys' p.224
13. Stephen Wright EEB p.41-42. Coggins 'John Smyth's Congregation' p.77-84. The Waterlander Mennonite Association was called the Broederschap. There

were tensions within the Association which the application brought to the surface. It isn't clear whether the 1610 application was for Smyth's congregation to join the Broederschap as a separate congregation (Coggins) or whether the problem was the large number of new and English members joining the Amsterdam congregation and thus distorting its character (Wright).

14. Stephen Wright EEB p.43
15. Known as 'A declaration of faith of English people remaining at Amsterdam in Holland.' This is reproduced in Burgess 'Smyth, Helwys' p.212-219. Burgess says there is an original copy in York Minster library. A copy of this declaration of faith can be found through Google. Type in the full title of the 'declaration of faith' and it will take you to the relevant page on the Evangelical Arminians website.
16. Proposition 83, found in Burgess 'Smyth, Helwys' p.255
17. Whitley 'Works' p.113
18. 'The Last Book' of John Smyth's can be found in Burgess 'Smyth, Helwys' p.257ff and Whitley 'Works' p.753ff
19. Jason Lee 'Theology of John Smyth' p.94. Coggins 'John Smyth's Congregation' p.167 says that Thomas Pygott published 'The Last Book'
20. Helwys in 'An Advertisement' (Burgess, 'Smyth, Helwys' p.230) claims that Smyth is apostate, and that having once been enlightened he cannot be restored again. (Hebrews 6:4-6) Smyth, understandably, took exception to this!
21. Stephen Wright EEB p.40
22. Burgess 'Smyth, Helwys' p.237
23. Burgess 'Smyth, Helwys' p.270-272. The date of admission was January 21st 1615. In the end about 4 of Smyth's congregation could not agree to join the Mennonites.
24. Jason Lee 'Theology of John Smyth' p.95: "The group met separately from 1615-1640 under Thomas Pygott, but was a part of the Dutch congregation. After Pygott's death, the English group faded into the other church." Whitley 'British Baptists' p.55 provides a little more detail: "When Piggott died in 1639 he was succeeded as minister at the bake-house by Joseph Drew, and when he died in 1642 a fourth Englishman was not available."
25. Coggins 'John Smyth's Congregation' p.110-111 points out that Smyth in his 'Last Book' was defending himself against accusations made by Helwys which only appeared in 'Mystery of Iniquity.' Smyth must have been acquainted with the contents of that book.
26. Burgess 'Smyth, Helwys' p.276-277
27. Whitley 'History of British Baptists' p.33
28. "That the magistrate is not by virtue of his office to meddle with religion, or matters of conscience, to force and compel men to this or that form of religion or doctrine; but to leave Christian religion free, to every man's conscience, and to handle only civil transgressions (Rom.xiii), injuries and wrongs of man against man, in murder, adultery, theft etc, for Christ only is the king, and

lawgiver of the church and conscience (James iv.12)" Proposition 84, in Burgess 'Smyth, Helwys' p.255

29. Smyth himself, in keeping with many of his contemporaries, had advocated this role for the magistrate in his earlier writings: "Magistrates should cause all men to worship the true God, or else punish them with imprisonment, confiscation of goods, or death as the qualitie of the cause requireth." 'A Paterne of True Prayer' quoted in Jason Lee 'The Theology of John Smyth' p.256

30. 'Short Declaration' ed. Richard Groves p.37

31. 'Short Declaration' ed. Richard Groves p.53

32. Whitley 'History of the British Baptists' p.33: "Smyth had enunciated the doctrine plainly in his 84th Proposition, but this was not yet issued in print."

33. Whitley 'History of British Baptists' p.33-34; Stephen Wright EEB p.39 & p.56

34. Jason Lee 'The Theology of John Smyth' p.274ff

35. Wright EEB p.57. See also McBeth 'English Baptist Literature' p.20

36. 'Short Declaration' ed. Richard Groves p.149

37. 'Short Declaration' ed. Richard Groves p.151

38. 'Short Declaration' ed. Richard Groves p.154

39. 'The Works of John Robinson' vol. 3 p.157

40. 'The Works of John Robinson' vol.3 p.159

41. Coggins 'John Smyth's Congregation' puts this well: "The Helwys congregation was left as a tiny group, friendless in a foreign land." p.102

42. Coggins 'John Smyth's Congregation' p.148.

43. Coggins 'John Smyth's Congregation' p.128: Helwys "may have risked his life in returning to England partly in order to be with his wife."

44. "When Bancroft died and was succeeded by Archbishop Abbot, a Puritan Anglican, Thomas Helwys and his people returned to England and settled in London." From an anonymous paper found in the 'John Smyth' file in the EMBA Archive, Market Harborough I suspect the author was the former archivist, T.J.Budge.

45. Whitley BQ vii 1934-35 p.251

46. Stephen Wright EEB p.46

47. Burgess 'Smyth, Helwys' p.281; Whitley 'British Baptists' p.34; Whitley BQ vol. vii p.252

48. Richard Groves in the introduction to his 1998 reproduction of 'Mystery of Iniquity' p.xxiv. By contrast, Burgess 'Smyth' Helwys' p.278 says that Helwys "put his book to the press in Holland and probably saw it completed before he left that country."

49. Coggins 'John Smyth's Congregation' p.170. The list given on page 170 includes the name of Joan Helwys. This seems anomalous since Coggins states that one of Helwys' motives in returning to England was to see his wife again. I have checked this with James Coggins who tells me that he included her because he believed she would have been part of his congregation in England.

50. Jason Lee 'The Theology of John Smyth' p.286

51. Richard Groves in his edition of the 'Mystery of Iniquity' p.xxiv
52. www.exlibris.org/nonconform/engdis/barrowists.html
53. Whitley 'British Baptists' p.35. See also Burrage 'Early English Dissenters' (EED) p.257
54. W.K.Jordan 'Development of Religious Toleration' vol.2 p. 265
55. 'The Works of John Robinson' vol.3 p.156
56. Adam Taylor 'History of the General Baptists' vol.1 p.91-95
57. Stephen Wright EEB p.45-46
58. Transactions of BHS vol.iii 1912/13 p.20
59. A version of the text is printed at the end of this chapter along with a facsimile of the original document which is still available in the Parliamentary archives. The document is dated <u>1613.</u> It is important to differentiate between this brief note called 'A Humble Supplication' and a much longer piece of a similar title produced perhaps in 1620 which tradition says was written by John Murton. Murton is supposed to have written the work in milk and had it smuggled out of prison as the milk bottle stoppers! This latter, longer work was reproduced in 'Tracts on Liberty of Conscience' in 1846. Champlin Burrage was dubious about its authenticity.
60. Burrage EED p.255
61. Burgess 'Smyth, Helwys' p.281
62. Burrage EED p.257
63. Collinson 'Elizabethan Puritan Movement' p.388
64. Collinson 'Elizabethan Puritan Movement' p.412-413: "The ingenuity of Barrow and Greenwood turned the Fleet into a clandestine publishing house at this very time, and the Puritan ministers enjoyed the same latitude, which was no more characteristic of Elizabethan prison life..... Even Cartwright, who could not safely be allowed this privilege, was permitted visits from his wife and those who had 'necessary business' with him."
65. J.T.Crozier 'Some notable women in Baptist History'
66. Coggins 'John Smyth's Congregation' p.170
67. Burgess 'Smyth, Helwys' p.225
68. Whitley 'British Baptists' p.31
69. Ernest Payne 'Thomas Helwys and the first Baptist Church' p.15
70. Burgess 'Smyth, Helwys' p.298-299
71. Coggins 'John Smyth's Congregation' p.35 states that Thomas Pygott may well have been a clergyman. Coggins also lists other members of the Pygott family on pages 33-36 and 162-163.

To the right Honorable assembly of the Commons House of Parliament

A most humble supplication of divers poor prisoners, and many others the King's native loyal subjects ready to testify it by the oath of allegiance in all sincerity, whose grievances are lamentable, only for the cause of conscience.

Most humbly showing that whereas in the Parliament holden in the seventh year of the King's majesty's reign that now is, it was enacted that all persons whatsoever above the age of eighteen years of age, not coming to Church etc. should take the oath of allegiance, and for the refusal thereof, should be committed to prison without bail etc. By such statute the Popish Recusants upon taking the oath, are daily delivered from imprisonments: and divers of us are also set at Liberty when we fall under the hands of the Reverend Judges and Justices. But when we fall into the hands of the bishops we can have no benefit by the said oath, for they say it belongeth only to Popish Recusants and not to others; but kept have we been by them in lingering imprisonments, divided from wives, children, servants and callings, not for any other cause but only for conscience toward God, to the utter undoing of us, our wives and children.

Our most humble supplication therefore to this high and Honorable Assembly is, that in commiseration of the distressed estate of us, our poor wives and children, it may be enacted in express words that other the King's majesty's faithful subjects, as well as the Romish Recusants may be freed from imprisonment upon taking the said oath.

And we shall still (as we do day and night) pray that the God of heaven may be in your Honorable Assembly, for by him do princes decree justice.

By his majesty's faithful subjects
Most falsely called
Anabaptists.

84

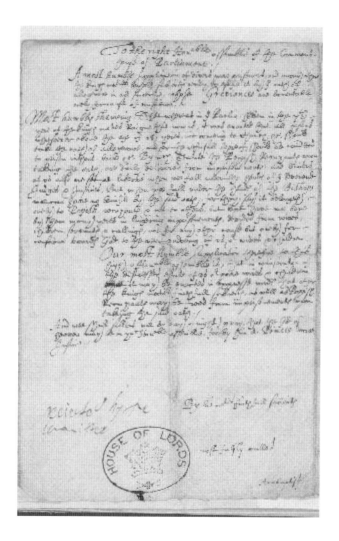

Copy of the original 'Most Humble Supplication' located in the parliamentary archives. It is dated 1613. A note with the document indicates that the petition was rejected. I am most grateful to Jennifer Lynch for locating this and making it available.

85

CHAPTER 7

ASSESSMENT, CONCLUSIONS AND HISTORICAL LEGACY

In 1624 the London Baptist Church led by John Murton began to exhibit tensions that led to the excommunication of sixteen of its members led by Elias Tookey.[1] Tookey wrote to the Waterlander Mennonites, still led by Hans de Ries, and formally requested that his sixteen members be recognised as a second Baptist Church and be brought into fellowship with the Waterlanders.[2] The request was eventually declined on the grounds that the origins of Elias Tookey's congregation were disorderly. There were also question marks regarding how this break away group understood the deity of Christ.[3]

Meanwhile Murton's congregation were themselves in communication with the Mennonites regarding association. Of enormous significance is a letter addressed to Hans de Ries and delivered by two of Murton's emissaries. The letter is from "the churches of Jesus Christ in England living in London, Lincoln, Sarum (Salisbury), Coventry and Tiverton (in Devon)."[4] Quite clearly by 1626 a network of Baptist churches was in existence, sharing at least some wide degree of belief. These congregations may have existed as Separatist conventicles before they were persuaded by the arguments of the Baptists. Coggins is struck by the fact that Lincoln was one of the five churches listed, and that John Smyth was from Lincoln. The suggestion is that Smyth had probably maintained correspondence with, and channelled his literature through, contacts in Lincoln.[5]

The five churches' approach for closer union with the Mennonites foundered eventually on one of the issues that had caused the rift in the first place: magistracy.[6] The English Baptist Churches sufficiently reflected Thomas Helwys' ideas. They could not abandon their belief in the right of Christians to bear arms and to serve in civil administration. It was to be one of the enduring differences between Continental Anabaptism and the English Baptists.

Barrie White wondered if the Helwys – Murton congregation formed the nucleus of the London congregation which was sending out evangelists to the Home Counties in the 1640s.[7] James Coggins is certainly of the mind that the Helwys – Murton congregation grew into the General Baptist denomination.[8] He expresses amazement that the ten people who arrived in England in 1612 should, against all the odds, be responsible for such a fruitful spiritual harvest. In that regard Helwys managed to trump John Smyth who in his desire for union with the Mennonites had effectively lost his sense of mission. "By committing the act of folly of returning to a nation that was determined to destroy him" Thomas Helwys and his handful of followers "won numerous converts and founded a denomination."[9]

That denomination was committed to a belief in general atonement. In 1620 John Murton published 'A description of what God hath predestinated'[10] in which he attacked the central tenets of Calvinism: predestination and perseverance.

"Can anything be more repugnant to the nature of God or more defacing his justice than to say that God punishes man with the torments of hell in everlasting fire for doing those things which he himself hath predestined, ordained, decreed, determined, appointed, willed and compelled him to do."

Murton was willing to acknowledge God as the "principal cause and author of all good." But he would not endorse the view that God somehow was the cause of that which was evil in the world. God did not make it a necessity that Adam should sin, and surrounded Adam with every incentive not to sin.

In laying out his position in this way Murton was clearly echoing the ideas of Helwys. But he made a significant shift away from Helwys and back towards Smyth over the vexed issue of free will. Murton insisted "that there is left in man the faculty of will, to choose or refuse." "What can be more plain that man hath free choice to work with God, or against God, in the work of his grace."[11] In thus repositioning the General Baptists in line with John Smyth's teaching, Murton was preserving some valuable insights that would prevent the complete hegemony of the Calvinistic Baptists, and would eventually contribute to a renewed theological and missiological awakening.

Thomas Helwys' writings make uncomfortable reading. Burgess tells us, "He was well versed in the Scriptures, but he lacked the sense of proportion which a wider range of reading would have given."[12] That is to put things mildly. Helwys' pen was vicious. He assaulted his opponents and saw no possible good in anyone with whom he disagreed. J.Glenwood Clayton is certainly right when he says that Helwys did not always reflect "the ideal Christian virtues, especially in his rigid dogmatism and readiness to condemn those of opposing viewpoint."[13] Some of this could be explained by the vital importance attached to these issues, and the passionate conviction that follows from the discovery of something new. The nature of the Church covenant itself may well have contributed not only to the strengthening of religious ties but also the vehemence of the language used when that covenant was broken.[14]

Thomas Helwys today is heralded as one of the first champions of religious liberty[15] and religious tolerance. His name is ever associated with those eloquent and purple passages in 'Mystery of Iniquity' which connect to our modern delight in human freedom.[16] And yet in Thomas Helwys there was a regrettable dissonance; a conflict between theory and practice. Helwys never seemed to make the connection between his high toned appeal to the King for freedom of expression, and his intemperate denunciation of those who expressed any views which were contrary to his own. It was left to others to make a more coherent and fulsome defence of religious liberty.

John Murton, for example, was to carry the tradition on in his work of 1615 'Objections answered by way of dialogue.' The Preface of that work notes that it is "heinous .... in the sight of the Lord to force men and women by cruel persecutions, to bring their bodies to a worship whereunto they cannot bring their spirits."[17]

But the man who was to give to the doctrine of absolute religious liberty "a full, critical and reasonably objective presentation"[18] was Leonard Busher.

Busher was born in Wotton under Edge, Gloucestershire about 1573.[19] He left for the Netherlands in about 1606 just before the Scrooby – Gainsborough group made their journey. Stephen Wright thinks it likely "that he was one of those re-baptized by Smyth in 1609."[20] Busher's name, however, does not appear on the list of those who applied to join the Mennonites in 1610, and it is more than likely that Busher had parted company with both Smyth and Helwys and formed a third group of English Baptists in Amsterdam.[21]

In 1614 Busher produced a work entitled 'Religion's Peace.' , It was the first ever Baptist treatise devoted exclusively to the theme of religious liberty.[22] Persecution, says Busher "is wholly against the mind and merciful law of Christ, dangerous to both king and state, a means to decrease the kingdom of Christ and a means to increase the kingdom of Antichrist."[23]

There were some very practical reasons why persecution was ill advised. "Though some men and women believe not at the first hour, yet may they at the eleventh hour, if they be not persecuted to death before."[24] Moreover, persecution invariably leads to hypocrisy. How can you be sure someone is sincere in their religious beliefs if those beliefs are borne of persecution?

Busher believed that truth was very important. But he was quite sure that "error and heresy cannot be killed by fire and sword but by the word and Spirit of God."[25] All compulsion in religion must be removed. People must be allowed to discover truth freely. And for those who remain obdurate in error then only persuasion can be employed.

W.K.Jordan, in his monumental four volume study of the development of religious toleration in England, sees the Baptists in general and Leonard Busher in particular as pioneers in the cause of religious freedom.

"Busher's most significant contribution is to be found in his attempt to justify a system of complete religious liberty on the basis of spiritual necessity and abstract right. Underlying his reasoning was the deep-rooted conviction that religious persecution was in fact anti-Christian .... Some body of Christians must champion this principle and call a halt to the hideous bigotry and bloodshed which have for so long engulfed Christendom, and he clearly felt that this should be the supreme contribution of his own sect."[26]

Jordan makes the important point that there is in the writings of Smyth, Helwys, Murton and Busher an intimate connection between their Arminianism and their commitment to religious liberty.[27] It is a point that has been repeated by more recent contributors.[28] If men and women are not predetermined to eternal life or death then they are possessed of sufficient freedom to respond to the offer of life in Jesus Christ. Such freedom is the lynchpin to salvation, and there can be no salvation without such freedom. Coercion, compulsion and conformity are consequently the enemy of true religion. One freedom is dependant on a second freedom.

In major studies of Stuart England Thomas Helwys rarely finds a mention. His writings scarcely attracted any interest at the time[29] and the lack of precise knowledge surrounding the last few years of his life serve as a reminder that his life passed with little note among his contemporaries. Today, Thomas Helwys is remembered through the 'Helwys Hall' at Regent's Park College, Oxford, and the Thomas Helwys Baptist Church in Nottingham. It is rightly observed that Helwys formed the first Baptist Church on English soil; made one of the first defences of religious liberty in the English language; and pioneered a uniquely English concept of Baptist Church polity with its acceptance of magistracy, and participation in the civil administration of the land.

Yet in so many things Helwys was indebted to his mentor John Smyth.[30] Writing in 1611 in his 'Declaration of faith of people remaining in Amsterdam' Helwys acknowledged not only the enormous debt he owed Smyth but also the great affection with which Smyth had been held:

"Yes, what would we not have endured or done? Would we not have lost all we had? Yes, would we not have plucked out our eyes? Would we not have laid down our lives? Doth not God know this? Do not men know it? Doth not he know it? Have we not neglected ourselves, our wives, our children and all we had and respected him? And we confess we had good cause so to do in respect of those most excellent gifts and graces of God that then did abound in him. And all our love was too little for him and not worthy of him."[31]

It was Smyth who convinced Helwys to leave the Church of England; it was Smyth who convinced Helwys to become a Baptist; it was Smyth who convinced Helwys to abandon Calvinism for Arminianism; it was Smyth who introduced Helwys to notions of religious liberty. While Thomas Helwys developed and modified some of these ideas, and in one aspect at least moved away from his mentor, it was John Smyth who truly deserves the label of Baptist pathfinder.[32]

John Smyth has not always been appreciated. A rather churlish entry in the Concise Dictionary of National Biography says of Smyth, "his religious views and tracts" were "incoherent and distracted".[33] This is hardly fair. Mandell Creighton was to make a more informed assessment of John Smyth's character and contribution to ecclesiastical history:

"None of the English Separatists had a finer mind or a more beautiful soul than John Smyth. None of them succeeded in expressing with so much reasonableness and consistency their aspirations after a spiritual system of religious beliefs and practice. None of them founded their opinions on so large and liberal a basis."[34]

Whitley maintained that "the cause of Separatism .... gained from him impulse sufficient to carry it on for a generation till it stood firm."[35] James Tull, who questioned the connection between Smyth and the General Baptists later in the century, still regarded him as one of the major 'Shapers of Baptist Thought'.[36]

This being so, I am still struck by the tremendous influence on Smyth (and on Helwys) played by the Dutch Anabaptists. Smyth's

92

Arminianism and his commitment to religious liberty can all be traced to well worn paths within Continental Anabaptism. The irenic spirit of his last writings (which more than any others attracted admiration of contemporary and subsequent commentators) can undoubtedly be attributed to the Anabaptist Mennonites. Helwys, Murton, Busher, and later Roger Williams, all espoused the cause of religious liberty that had been well worked through eighty years before by Balthasar Hubmaier.[37] The Baptists may have been the first Christian group to advocate and expound the need for full religious freedom, but it was the Continental not the English Baptists who made this connection first. Attempts to trace English Baptist origins to sources other than the European scene[38] fly in the face of the natural evidence.

That the Baptists were the first to defend and promote full religious liberty is not something that would be apparent today. Baptists during the twentieth century became more concerned with discerning and defending 'truth.' Doctrinal purity and evangelical orthodoxy became more important than tolerating theological diversity. As a denomination the Baptists have been scared to associate themselves with liberal positions for fear of alienating more conservative elements. Tolerance of the rights of religious minorities has been hesitant and uncertain for many Baptists who are often oblivious to their own roots, and are fearful of the religious strength of others.

Curiously, the adoption of believers' baptism, which today is considered the major contribution of Smyth and Helwys, was not the major concern of either man in their writings.[39] They were consumed with far wider and deeper theological battles. John Smyth regarded the rejection of predestination, the questioning of original sin, the promotion of free will, and the defence of religious liberty as part of an exciting and liberating agenda.

Jason Lee is probably right when he says that "the catalyst for Smyth's change is a new understanding of the extensiveness of God's love."[40] Such a transformative discovery many Christians need to experience today as well. There is always a tendency to "make His love too narrow by false limits of our own" and to "magnify His strictness with a zeal He will not own."[41]

John Smyth, Thomas Helwys and John Robinson committed themselves to "walk in all His ways made known, or to be made known unto them."[42]They were to discover that "The Lord hath yet more light and truth to set forth from His Word."[43] As Christians in the twenty first century we need to be open to that same attitude of mind; to be willing to embrace those with markedly differing views to our own; and to comprehend the enormous breadth of the love of God which far surpasses all our feeble attempts to define it.

Footnotes

1. Stephen Wright 'Early English Baptists' p.61
2. Whitley 'British Baptists' p.46
3. Stephen Wright 'Early English Baptists' p.61
4. Burrage 'Early English Dissenters'
5. Coggins 'John Smyth's Congregation' p.107
6. Burgess 'Smyth, Helwys' p.335
7. Barrie White 'English Separatist Tradition' p.165; Barrie White 'English Baptists of 17th Century' p.29: "While there is no certain evidence that the London Church of General Baptists persisted through the difficult years of the 1630s it seems reasonable to believe that the Bell Alley congregation of the 1640s was in the direct succession of those who had returned with Thomas Helwys."
8. Coggins 'John Smyth's Congregation' p.107
9. Coggins 'John Smyth's Congregation' p.150
10. A brief account of this work can be found in Burgess 'Smyth, Helwys' p.311ff and Wright 'Early English Baptists' p.52ff. The full text is available at the Angus Library in Regents Park College, Oxford.
11. Stephen Wright 'Early English Baptists' p.53
12. Burgess 'Smyth, Helwys' p.203
13. J.Glenwood Clayton 'Thomas Helwys: a Baptist Founding Father' BHH vol. viii p.15
14. Coggins 'John Smyth's Congregation' p.120. "When a split came it produced the rancor of a divorce because the covenant had all the force of a wedding vow."
15. Alec Gilmore writing in The Guardian, Saturday May 20th 2006
16. Brian Haymes article 'On Religous Liberty' in BQ vol.42 July 2007
17. H.Leon McBeth 'English Baptist Literature on Religious Liberty to 1689' (EBL) p.51. McBeth uses the text of Murton's work and Busher's 'Religion's Peace' , made available in the 1846 Hanserd Knollys 'Tracts on Liberty of Conscience and persecution' edited by E.B.Underhill. It should be pointed out that Stephen Wright (EEB p.45) believes that Thomas Helwys was responsible for 'Objections' and not Murton.

18. W.K.Jordan 'The Development of Religious Toleration in England' vol.2 p.296
19. Stephen Wright BQ vol. 39 October 2001: 'Leonard Busher: Life and ideas' p.175
20. Stephen Wright BQ p.176
21. Stephen Wright BQ p.176. The evidence for this is in a letter of 8th July 1611 in which Matthew Saunders and Cuthbert Hutten, former members of the Ancient Church, reported the presence in Amsterdam of "Maister Smith an Anabaptist of one sort, and maister Helwys of another, and maister Busher of another."
22. H.Leon McBeth EBL p.39
23. H.Leon McBeth EBL p.43
24. H.Leon McBeth EBL p.43
25. H.Leon McBeth EBL p.44
26. W.K.Jordan DRT p.297
27. W.K.Jordan DRT p.261-262: "The Baptists had discovered the firmest grounds for claiming liberty of conscience when they held 'that conscience is the organ of an inner light which comes from God.' Men who were convinced that all necessary truth in religion would be revealed to any man who soberly and sincerely sought for it would view with the greatest disfavour any interference in the complete freedom of the relationship of man with his God. This theory they held not only for themselves but as an abstract principle of religious truth."
28. A.C.Underwood 'A History of the English Baptists' p.49; H.Leon McBeth EBL p.43: "That Arminians rather than Calvinists first advocate absolute religious liberty was not accidental."
29. Barrie White ('Biographical Dictionary of British Radicals in the 17th Century' ed. Greaves and Zaller 1984) says of Helwys' 'Mystery of Iniquity', "there is no evidence that it enjoyed either a wide influence or a wide circulation at the time, nor was it ever, as far as is known, reprinted in the seventeenth century. So its contemporary influence was of the slightest." Walter Burgess ('Smyth, Helwys p.225) observes that Helwys' 'A short and plain proof' (1611) did not excite "any special notice in England."
30. W.R. Estep 'The Anabaptist Story' p.224-225
31. Quoted in Jason Lee 'The Theology of John Smyth' p.95 and Walter Burgess 'Smyth, Helwys' p.208
32. A.C.Underwood 'History of the English Baptists' p.44 referred to Smyth as a pathfinder. James E. Tull 'Shapers of Baptist Thought' p.30 picked up that phrase from Underwood.
33. OUP 1992
34. The Mandell Creighton quote is in Whitley 'Works of John Smyth' p.118 and Underwood 'History of the English Baptists' p.45
35. Whitley 'Works of John Smyth' p.118
36. 'Shapers of Baptist Thought' was first published in 1972 and reprinted in 1984.

37. W.R.Estep 'The Anabaptist Story' p.225ff makes this connection with Hubmaier and the later exponents of religious liberty.

38. Coggins 'John Smyth's Congregation' p.23 points out that Whitley seemed particularly keen to see the English origins of Baptist ecclesiology especially after the First World War had fractured relations with Continental Europe. Barrie White has strenuously attempted to locate Baptist thought within an English rather than a Continental milieu.

39. Coggins 'John Smyth's Congregation' p.106

40. Jason Lee 'The Theology of John Smyth' p.201

41. From the hymn 'There's a wideness in God's mercy' by F.W.Faber: 573 in 'Baptist Praise and Worship'

42. William Bradford 'of Plymouth Plantation' p.8

43. From the hymn 'We limit not the truth of God to our poor reach of mind' by George Rawson: 107 in 'Baptist Praise and Worship'. The words that 'the Lord had more truth and light to break forth from His holy Word' were used, according to Edward Winslow, by John Robinson as his final spoken encouragement to the Pilgrim Fathers. The full quotation is provided in David Beale 'The Mayflower Pilgrims' p.87

BIBLIOGRAPHY

Allan, Sue, 'Lady Rose Hickman' (Domtom Publishing 2009)

Allan, Sue, 'Tudor Rose' (Domtom Publishing 2009)

Anwyl, E. Catherine, 'John Smyth the Se-Baptist' (Gainsborough 1991)

Babbage, Stuart, 'Puritanism and Richard Bancroft' (London 1962)

Bangs, Jeremy, 'The Pilgrims, Leiden and the early years of Plymouth Plantation' (online publication: google the full title)

Beale, David, 'The Mayflower Pilgrims' (Ambassador Productions 2000)

Bradford, William, 'Of Plymouth Plantation' (Modern Library Edition 1981)

Burgess, Walter, 'John Smith, Thomas Helwys and the first Baptist Church in England' (London 1911)

Burgess, Walter, 'Transactions of the Baptist Historical Society' vol.III 1912-13

Burrage, Champlin, 'The Early English Dissenters' (1912)

Cheetham, J.Keith, 'On the Trail of the Pilgrim Fathers' (Luath Press 2001)

Clayton, J.Glenwood, 'Thomas Helwys: a Baptist Founding Father' (in 'Baptist History and Heritage' vol.VIII Jan.1973)

Collinson, Patrick, 'The Elizabethan Puritan Movement' (London 1967)

Collinson, Patrick, 'Archbishop Grindal' (London 1979)

Crosby, Thomas, 'The History of the English Baptists' vol. I (first published, London 1738; reprinted in Arkansas by the Baptist Standard Bearer inc. as part of their Baptist History Series, vol.16)

Coggins, James, 'John Smyth's Congregation' (Herald Press 1991)

Crozier, J.T. 'Some notable women in Baptist History' (Dunedin, N.Z. 1930s)

Dexter H.M. & M., 'The England and Holland of the Pilgrims' (1905)

Estep, William, 'The Anabaptist Story' (Eerdmans 1975)

Gill, Crispin, 'The Mayflower Remembered' (Newton Abbot 1970)

Haller, William, 'The Rise of Puritanism' (Columbia University Press 1938)

Harrison, Fred, 'The Nottinghamshire Baptists' vol.I unpublished M.Phil, Nottingham University 1972

Haymes, Brian, 'On Religious Liberty: re-reading *A Short Declaration of the Mystery of Iniquity*' Baptist Quarterly 42, July 2007

Helwys, Thomas, 'A Short Declaration of the Mystery of Iniquity' (edited by Richard Groves, Mercer University Press, 1998)

Heaton, Vernon, 'The Mayflower' (Exeter 1980)

Jessup, Edmund, 'The Mayflower Story' (Retford 1977)

Jordan, W.K. 'The Development of Religious Toleration in England' vol.2 (London 1932-1940)

Klaassen, Walter, 'Anabaptism:neither Catholic nor Protestant' (Conrad 1981)

Klassen, William & Klaassen, Walter (eds.), 'The Writings of Pilgram Marpeck' (Herald Press 1978)

Lee, Jason, 'The Theology of John Smyth' (Mercer University Press 2003)

Marchant, Ronald, 'The Puritans and the Church Courts 1560-1642' (Longmans 1960)

McBeth, H.Leon, 'English Baptist Literature on Religious Liberty'   (Arno Press 1980)

Murton, John, 'A description of what God hath predestinated' (1620)

Payne, Ernest, 'Thomas Helwys and the first Baptist Church in England' (BUGB 1966)

Randall, Ian M. 'Communities of Conviction' (European Baptist Federation 2009)

Robinson, John, 'The Works' vol.3 (edited by Robert Ashton 1851)

Taylor, Adam, 'History of the General Baptists' vol.1 (1818)

Tull, James E. 'Shapers of Baptist Thought' (Mercer University Press 1984)

Underwood, A.C. 'History of the English Baptists' (London 1947)

Vernon, Jennifer, 'Gainsborough Old Hall and the Mayflower Pilgrim Story' (Gainsborough 1991)

Vedder, Henry C. 'Balthasar Hubmaier: the leader of the Anabaptists' (1905: reproduced by Kessinger publishing as part of their *Legacy reprint series)*

Wenger, J.W.(ed.), 'Complete Writings of Menno Simons' (Herald Press 1984)

White, B.R. 'The English Separatist Tradition' (Oxford University Press 1971)

White, B.R. 'English Baptists of 17th Century' (Baptist Historical Society 1983)

Whitley, W.T. 'The Works of John Smyth' (1915)

Whitley, W.T. 'History of the British Baptists' (London 1923)

Whitley, W.T. 'Thomas Helwys of Gray's Inn' Baptist Quarterly 7, 1934

Wood, J.H. 'Condensed History of General Baptists' (1847)

Wright, Stephen, 'The Early English Baptists 1603-1649' (Boydell Press 2006)

Wright, Stephen, 'Leonard Busher: life and ideas' Baptist Quarterly 39, 2001

INDEX